TO BE
DISPOSED
BY
AUTHORITY

THE HOME UNIVERSITY LIBRARY
OF MODERN KNOWLEDGE

· 196 ·

THE WEALTH OF ENGLAND
FROM 1496 TO 1760

THE
WEALTH OF ENGLAND
FROM 1496 TO 1760

G. N. CLARK

GEOFFREY CUMBERLEGE
OXFORD UNIVERSITY PRESS
LONDON   NEW YORK   TORONTO
1946

PRINTED IN GREAT BRITAIN
8245.

CONTENTS

PREFACE

As this book has no references to authorities except for the bibliography at the end, I ought to say that although some parts of it are new, in some others I have accepted the conclusions of previous writers. If I have anywhere followed their words more closely than is proper without using quotation-marks, I have done it inadvertently, and ask pardon. I must express my sincere thanks to my friends Miss Lynda Grier and Mr. F. R. Salter, who have most kindly read the book in 'typescript' and made very helpful comments.

G. N. C.

CAMBRIDGE.
17 *September* 1945

CHAPTER I

ENGLISH ECONOMY AT
THE 'END OF THE MIDDLE AGES'

ECONOMIC history traces through the past the matters with which economics is concerned. These are the thoughts and acts of men and women in those relations which have to do with their work and livelihood, such relations as those of buyers and sellers, producers and consumers, town-dwellers and countrymen, rich and poor, borrowers and lenders, masters and men or, as we say nowadays, employers and employees, and unemployed too. In economic history there is never a definite starting-point. However far we go back into the past, we have to do with men who worked along with their fathers, in an economic world which was already a going concern when they were born, until the older generation dropped out and their own sons were working beside them. If we were to go back to palaeolithic times we should be dealing with a very experienced world in which there had been many changes and in which new practices were growing up while others were obsolescent. This little book will therefore begin in the middle of the story, as we all have to begin our lives in the middle of it; it will begin at a selected point of time, without leading up to it through the previous ages, which indeed were almost altogether unknown to the people then living.

The point at which we begin is the year 1496, when King Henry VII had been eleven years on the throne, when the authority of the Catholic Church was still unchallenged, and when no one had yet reached

America or India from an English port. The boundaries of the kingdom were then pretty much what they are now, including Wales, but not including Scotland, though in some ways the king's Welsh subjects were still treated as foreigners in England. The population was a mere fraction, perhaps a twelfth, of what it has since become. No one has yet made a close, scientific estimate of the population at the end of the fifteenth century. The conjectures of historians vary between four millions and less than two millions and a half, and on the whole they agree that at this time the total population was not changing rapidly, but was pretty well stationary.

Most of the inhabitants worked on the land, and in the matter of food the country supported itself and did no more. Corn and butter and cheese were indeed exported from time to time, but this does not mean that the country had a regular surplus of food. Even with the small square-rigged ships of that time, transport by sea, in spite of its risks, was cheaper, as it always is, than transport by land, and so corn might be shipped from Hull or Yarmouth to Holland when there was a shortage in the west Midlands. In another year corn would be imported into England when it was more abundant, and therefore, cheaper, on the Continent. Our seaborne trade in food sufficed only to mitigate temporary shortages, generally after bad harvests. The only important exception was the importing of fish. Foreigners, especially from the Low Countries, regularly landed sea-fish in English ports. Some came from as far away as Iceland, but even those which were caught close to the English coasts must count as imports. The Dutch were skilled, as the English were not, in salting herrings, and these were welcome food in the eastern and south-eastern counties, especially in the winter, when there was no fresh produce on the farms. After this naturally lean time came the close season, the breeding time, for birds and animals, so that the Church, by insisting on fasting in Lent, did not make life much harder than it was bound to be.

The danger of shortage was never far distant, and sometimes there were famines; there might indeed be famine in one part of England and plenty in another. Inland transport was so expensive that the price of corn varied considerably from the areas where it was easiest to grow to those where it was most difficult: it was easy round the Upper Severn, and the Upper Thames, Cambridge and Bristol, and in East Suffolk, difficult in South Wales, East Essex, Durham and much of Yorkshire. There were producing areas and consuming areas, but the corn-trade moved mainly within regions of perhaps fifty miles, two or three days' journey, in diameter. The corn most easily grown in a locality was most in use there. Wheat was everywhere regarded as the best bread-corn, and was prescribed by the Church for the sacramental bread; but in the west and north, with their heavier rainfall and their hills and mountains, oatcake was the regular cereal food, and over most of the country much rye and barley-meal were baked. The nursery rhyme belongs to a later date than that we are dealing with, but we may quote it here:

> Sing a song of sixpence, a pocketful of rye,
> Four and twenty blackbirds baked in a pie.

They did eat blackbirds, as country people still some-times eat wheatears and missel-thrushes. They had to eat what they could get, and although sea-fish were more highly esteemed, they used fresh-water fish far more than we do: the abbot and the nobleman had their ponds for carp and pike; the fishing in the rivers was let out to fishermen, who brought salmon, trout, pike, perch, eels, and crayfish to market. We know that hot pies and bread and butter were ordinary English fare, and that the Londoner's Sunday joint was eaten cold during the week; we know that horse-flesh was regarded as carrion; but it is surprisingly hard to discover exactly what the different classes of people got to eat in different parts of the country. There was no winter feed for cattle except hay, and that was scarce, so in the autumn many cattle were slaughtered. The meat was salted and, with bacon, eggs, poultry, and game, had to serve till the grass grew again. It seems that vegetables were used mainly in soups and stews, and the chief vegetables were onions, garlic, leeks, and cabbages. On the whole they probably had a fairly good country diet, especially in milk, butter, and cheese, except for bad times. Modern dietitians suspect that they had not enough fats and vegetables, that all classes must have been in a state of sub-scurvy, and that perhaps a mild degree of 'vitamin A deficiency' was fairly common. But that is guesswork.

Foreign visitors regarded the English as a well-fed people. The great variety of soils and crops, of uplands and plains, no doubt partly accounted for this: a wet year was a bad year for the sheep and for the corn on the heavy clays, but there were lighter soils, even if they were smaller in extent, and there the enemy was drought. Variety meant that the food supplies did not all fail at once, and this was good for the country as a whole, because, as things then were, England was more fortunate than most parts of Europe in the matter of transport. All round the long and irregular coast there were harbours, hardly anywhere more than twenty miles apart, and many of them had useful jetties and breakwaters. A good part of the surface of England was within a day's journey of some port that could be reached by seagoing vessels. Many of these ports were deep in the most fertile districts. Where a river had its lowest bridge, generally near the top of the tide, there was a port like London, York, Norwich, Exeter, Bristol, or Chester, or a good many others, some of them far inland. Besides the ports for foreign or coastwise trade there were many navigable rivers. The Thames carried barges as far as Henley; the Great and Little Ouse, the Nene and the Cam made a wide area accessible from King's Lynn; half a dozen waterways flowed down to the Humber; the Severn and its two Avons carried the traffic of the Welsh border and part of the Midlands. Here and there the rivers had been improved by man; but many of them were blocked by weirs and other obstructions from which millers and fishermen made their living to the detriment of transport. It was only by river that bulky loads could be carried easily; but the pack-horses and two-wheeled carts which used the roads could handle corn and wool, and for some short hauls even building stone, at economic rates. There were ancient roads everywhere, good enough for the needs of the time, though some of them became impassable in the winter. Most of them were green roads wide enough to leave room to circumvent the mud; but a few were metalled and were kept in repair. There were hundreds of stone bridges, and more were being provided by pious donations or by tolls levied on the traffic. Movement was slow, so no perishables could be carried far.

Otherwise, since there was no need to keep to any time-table, slowness did not matter except that it was expensive in labour.

Over a large part of the country, including all the Midlands and parts of the south and north-east, the fully settled and cultivated land was laid out in the famous open-field system. In this arrangement, which showed endless variations in every detail, the peasants held their arable land in scattered strips; they had rights of common in some of the woods or heaths, in the permanent pastures, and over the stubble after harvest. 'Common-rights' played a considerable part in their lives, but there was very little of the communal in their organization. The arable land and its crops were the peasant's own. There was a village herdsman, but the cattle were owned individually. A village hayward looked after the common meadows, but when hay-time came they were divided into portions for which the peasants drew lots. Each cut and carried the hay from his own portion. It was impossible for one man to plough or sow or reap the intermixed strips at a very different time from another; and in many cases both the dates for these operations and the crops to be sown were prescribed by rigid custom; but this, and any co-operation there may have been, did not prevent the system from being essentially individualistic. One man prospered and another failed: they did not stand or fall together.

This open-field system had come down from immemorial antiquity. It was taken for granted; if its merits and defects were discussed, no record of the discussion from a date as early as 1496 has come down to us.[1] Within living memory in some places where

[1] But see p. 71, below.

fresh land had been taken in from forest or marsh and
brought under cultivation, it had been distributed in
the form of strips in new open fields. Perhaps this
was never done as late as 1496, and perhaps in the
fifteenth century it was done only where there were
already open fields to which additions could be made.
It seems doubtful whether English colonists in Ireland
(or later in America) carried the system with them.
Its vitality was gone, and in many places it was being
nibbled away. Where the produce of the land went
to market, whether it was corn or wool, or butter and
cheese, there might well be a motive for peasants to
exchange their strips and consolidate their holdings,
or for landowners, whether individuals or monasteries,
to buy out common rights over their land and so
acquire freedom to follow what methods of farming
they pleased. Such transactions were sometimes done
in a just and regular way, but sometimes the big men
merely robbed or defrauded the small. All this was
true also in the parts of England where there was no
open-field system. In these other parts there were
many different kinds of 'common of pasture', grazing
rights, especially over the uncultivated fells and moors;
but the holdings were more compact. They were of
innumerable shapes and sizes, and life was very
different in the rich villages of East Anglia and in the
scattered farms and hamlets of the northern and
western hills; but everywhere the land was peopled
in the main by peasants who worked it for their own
subsistence.

What was their economic position: on what terms
did they hold their land, from whom did they buy, to
whom did they sell, who were employers and who
were employed? Here again there was great variety,

but the answers to all these questions are in terms of individuals, not village communities. Every peasant had a landlord over him and every landlord had another landlord over his head unless they held directly from the supreme landlord, the king. The landlords were not all individuals; some of them, as now, were corporate bodies, such as deans and chapters or colleges, but their relation to their tenants, exercised through some such officer as a steward or bursar, was the same as if they had been individuals. In this multiple system of subordination of landholders to one another and to the king there were two kinds of links, an older and a newer, side by side. The older plan is sometimes called the feudal system, from *feudum*, the Latin word for a 'fief'. The king granted various rights, by no means the same in every case, over a particular stretch of land to one of his subjects or to a corporation, and this land was called a 'fief' or 'benefice' (the word we still use for ecclesiastical livings). It was the benefit conferred for certain services which were to be rendered: sometimes military service, sometimes the prayers of priests, sometimes official services in the administration, any sort of service, in fact, which the king needed. Those to whom the king granted land themselves in turn acted in the same way, conferring some of their rights in exchange for services. At the lowest stage the cultivator acquired the right to make his living from one holding of land. In consideration of this right, he had to work on the land which his landlord kept in hand and to give the lord from time to time some produce, such as eggs or nuts or, at rare intervals, a beast or some other necessary. Sometimes there were three or four intermediate landlords between the peasant and the king, though in a number of villages the king was the immediate landlord of the men who sowed and reaped. The immediate landlord, king or nobleman, commoner or corporation, was the lord of a 'manor', and so, from the point of view of the life of the country-side, the feudal system is called 'the manorial system'. A manor might be large or small; it might or might not have other manors within or below it; its essence was that it had a lord with rights over his tenants and, unless he were the king, with duties to his lord.

There were many variations in the rights of land-lords of all grades, but besides his own 'demesne' land the lord of the manor usually had other rights which enabled him to keep up his position. He owned the manorial mill, a watermill or windmill, where all corn had to be ground, the miller's services being paid for in corn or in money and the lord taking a share. He might have the sole right to keep pigeons, and the manorial dovecotes, of which many remain, were valuable both for food and for manure. There was a manorial court which enforced most of the rights and duties of the people concerned, the lord's steward presiding and the tenants forming the jury. By means of the court, the lord's power acted as a unifying force, supplementing the force of custom. The tenants were legally classified in many different types. The standard types were the freeholders and the villeins. Free-holders did not own their land outright quite as much as they do nowadays; they had to pay rent for it; but they could sell it, bequeath it by will if they did not want it to descend to their heirs, mortgage it, leave it, or neglect it. The villeins, which originally meant simply 'villagers', were, in their capacity of tenants, unfree, though they were far from being slaves and were often substantial men. The villein was supposed to be tied to the soil—that is, he had to live in the manor where his holding lay. If he took himself off, the manorial court made ineffective attempts to catch him. But this practice was dying out; it was restricted by a legal dictum of this year 1496, and in any case the villein had a right to his holding; his right was recorded in the rolls of the manorial court, and if a copy of the entry was given to him, he had a 'copy-hold'. The word 'villein' was, at or very soon after this time, giving place to the name 'tenant by copy of court roll' or simply 'copyholder'. Villeins and free-holders intermarried and regarded one another as equals: the legal distinction between them was not a social distinction.

In addition to the many kinds of landlords and tenants, there were also landless labourers who worked for wages in money or in kind. As at the present day, their numbers varied from place to place with the different types of farming: the smallest family farms could afford none and needed none, but there were some people nearly everywhere, such as the vicar, the miller, the smith, who might offer employment, and the bigger the scale of farming or the higher the pro-portion of goods that went to market, the greater was the division of labour and the more hired labourers there were. Altogether there were thousands of them, and there were laws, not very easily enforced, to prevent employers from competing for their services by offering more than a local maximum wage fixed by the justices of the peace, who were appointed from among the landlords.

The landless labourers formed an element alien to the general principle of the feudal or manorial system, the rewarding of services by granting a livelihood from land. But there were so many other exceptions that they constituted a second system alongside of the feudal system, the system of the 'cash nexus' or money tie. To work any estate satisfactorily, some regularity was necessary, and for centuries past there had been agreements, generally, though not always, embodied in legal documents, by which the services due to lords in their manors had been fixed. As demands for money in taxation and as buying and selling for money in markets extended, it suited many people to whom services or payments in kind were due to 'commute' them and take money instead. Equally, it suited those who owed services or payments in kind, especially if these were uncertain, to be quit of these obligations for fixed sums of money and to raise the money by selling their produce, thus venturing out from the comparatively limited opportunities of the manor into the more adventurous world of the produce markets, with their risks of loss and their chances of profit. Thus, all along the line, money relations became a new economic basis for agriculture. In the fifteenth century landlords took to letting their demesne farms on leases, so much land for such and such a time for so much rent. Therefore they no longer needed unpaid labour; they were willing to give the villeins documents enfranchising them, making the burdens of their copy-hold tenure certain and commercial in nature. The villeins were willing to pay the fees for these docu-ments, which gave them command over their own time and their produce, and so by 1496 there were very few villeins left in England. Although there was still an intricate web of feudal obligations entangling, as well as steadying, agricultural life, the newer system was emerging under which landless labourers worked for rent-paying farmers, who owned part of the equipment (or capital) of the farms, while the remainder, the buildings and fences, sometimes the animals (as is still the case on many sheep-farms), belonged to the landlord. Money economy was not a new invention; it had existed ever since there had been money; but its range was being greatly extended. We must remember, however, that contemporaries were not aware of the importance of this transition. Our knowledge of it comes not from any mention in the writings of the period, but from the studies of modern historians who have pieced together hundreds of unrelated local instances. The general character of agricultural life was that it moved slowly. It did not stand still, but it was traditional and conservative. The standard text-book of estate-management was still that of a thirteenth-century Dominican friar, Walter of Henley.

It is impossible to give any but the vaguest estimates of the numbers of the different social strata into which rural society was divided. To begin with, we do not know how many manors or villages and similar agricultural units there were, but there may have been something in the region of ten thousand. There were, at all events, almost that number of ecclesiastical parishes in England and Wales. These included, on the one hand, the numerous small parishes of the towns, of which London had 126, and on the other the vast areas of some of the northern parishes, like Halifax, reputed the largest, which was seventeen miles long and on an average eleven miles wide; but for the most part they coincided with the single agricultural settlements as country parishes do now. The largest individual landowner was the king, and no distinction was drawn between his public capacity as the head of the State and his private capacity as a landlord. The revenue from his many manors and miscellaneous dues had recently been increased by stricter, more efficient and more centralized administration, while the confiscations of the lands of rebels increased his possessions. The king's net revenue as landlord was probably now about £18,000 a year. In itself that figure tells us very little; but it is useful to compare it with some other figures.[1] The richest of King Henry's subjects was Sir William Stanley, and when his property was confiscated after he was condemned for treason, he appears to have been worth £9,000 in ready money and more than £1,000 a year in revenue from lands. The nobility, who in 1496 consisted only of about forty peers and their families, were men of perhaps between £500 and £1,000 a year. Below them, though not divided economically by a hard and fast line, came a great body of 'gentry'—a word not yet used in this sense—numbering altogether perhaps 9,000 or so, whom we may describe as squires, lords of manors. Their incomes varied from several hundred pounds in cash or kind or both to £10 a year. According to the law, everyone with more than £40 a year from land had to become a knight, thus acquiring a title of honour which involved the payment of certain taxes on a higher scale. The richer gentry were lords

[1] Throughout this book I have given figures of the public revenue and of typical incomes. These are useful for comparison provided we have an idea of how the different types of people lived. I have avoided comparisons of the purchasing-power of sums of money, such as a pound. Even when things bought at different periods were similar, their place in the whole outlay and consumption of the purchasers changed so much that the changes of prices did not mean that they were proportionately harder or easier to acquire.

of several manors which, if they were conveniently situated, they managed, as the king and the nobility did theirs, in groups. The smallest were lords of single manors. Their houses, when they survive to the present day, have often become farm-houses, but many are so small that to make comfortable farm-houses they have been added to at different times. The duties of all ranks were carefully graded according to income, not only for taxation, but also for military service, and below the gentry came the freeholders worth from 40s. to £10 a year, who had the parliamentary vote. Of these there were a good many thousands. Perhaps an even greater number of copyholders and tenant farmers, although voteless, were economically their equals. All this rural middle class, the stratum below the gentry, may be vaguely described as yeomanry.[1] Unfortunately, we do not know whether over the country as a whole they were more or less numerous than the wage-earning class of labourers.

Much land was owned by the Church. We do not know whether the once-current statements about the total amount were true or not. The only fairly definite fact is that in England alone (without Wales) 553 monastic houses in the year 1535 had a total net revenue of £135,000. In addition, there were friaries, bishops, deans and chapters, 'hospitals', and colleges of various kinds, besides the parish clergy, who lived by glebe lands and tithes, from which sources much also went to the monasteries and is not reckoned in the total just given. Altogether, then, the Church may have been drawing ten times as much from the land

[1] The excellent word 'yeoman' never designated any definite class: it was used in the towns as well as the country and, as now, in the Army and Navy, and for the Yeomen of the Guard.

as the king, or the State, but, of course, with the difference that the king's revenues were all his own, but the Church as such was not one landlord but an aggregate of more than ten thousand, from the bishops and mitred abbots who lived like great noblemen to the parish priests who lived little better than their copyholding neighbours.

The land represented the result of thousands of years of work and planning, which in some places had never been interrupted. The clearing of forests and moors and scrub, the draining of marshes and valleys had created a vast fixed capital, and this was preserved and managed by elaborate institutions which controlled the working of the landlords' authority and of money transactions. The reclaimed marshes give the best example. Romney Marsh, where the richest sheep pastures in the country were, was drained land, and the duties of the landowners in keeping up the ditches and embankments were enforced by a system of juries, which enlisted local co-operation and business capacity under royal authority in vigorous self-government. The 'custom of Romney Marsh' was in force also in parts of Yorkshire, Lincolnshire and elsewhere; and there were drained areas in the Fens, around the Thames Estuary, in Sedgemoor, in the Isle of Wight, and other parts. But what was obvious of these areas was more or less true of the whole cultivated area: it was made land, a fund of productive wealth formed by the investment of their surplus resources by countless individuals. Some of them were pioneers who added to their own holdings by the sweat of their brows; others were landowners who singly or in combination organized their hired men and tenants for larger works which would not repay them until many annual harvests had gone by. To create this productive wealth and to maintain it, countrymen of every station worked together as associates bound together by the law, by mutual aid, and by common sense.

Transport being what it was, the country-dweller found most of his necessaries much nearer home than we do now. His house was thatched with reeds or straw; he ate from a wooden platter; his ale was home-brewed from malt made in the village; the cloth for his hose and jerkin might be woven in the village from yarn spun by the womenfolk on the farm; but there were many things for which the country depended on towns. In England, as in western Europe generally, it was possible almost everywhere for the peasant from the most distant rural settlement to go to market in a town, do his business and be home by nightfall. The market-towns had not grown up at haphazard: the kings and lords had regulated their growth, taking care that they were not too close together nor too far apart. Their distribution was sparse or dense according to the population and needs of the district. In all England and Wales there were between 600 and 700. Of these Yorkshire, one-eighth of England in area, had less than fifty, but busy and populous Suffolk, with a quarter of the area of Yorkshire, had twenty-eight. Most of them were very small. London was in a class by itself with some 40,000 or 50,000 inhabitants. There were perhaps thirty towns or thereabouts with anything from 5,000 to 10,000: the best figure we have is for Coventry where, less than a generation after this date, the people were enumerated at 6,601, and Coventry was in all probability one of the twenty-five largest towns. Most even of these would by our standards not be urban in their appearance and scarcely urban in their ways of life: they had fields in which their burgesses could grow crops and turn out cattle, and they looked like large villages where a few hundred shopkeeper-craftsmen lived.

Town and country were not so sharply distinguished in England as they were on the Continent; but the towns had their own distinctive economic functions and organization. Their first business was to provide facilities for buying and selling, fairs and markets. There were some important periodical fairs in the open country, like the greatest of them all, Stourbridge fair just outside Cambridge, where every kind of English or foreign goods were sold, or the wool fair of the Golden Mile on the downs above East Hendred in Berkshire; but for the most part these gatherings were held in towns. According to the law, every fair was a market, but not every market was a fair: if there was a clear distinction, it was that fairs were larger than markets and were held only on a few stated days in the year, whereas markets were held once a week or oftener. In the ordinary weekly market of a small town the neighbouring farmers sold their surplus of produce and bought their implements or other small requirements. For the special seasonal markets or fairs, whether general or specially for cattle, sheep, or what not, buyers and sellers would come from distances greater or less according to the quantity and variety of the wares. The right to hold a market, like the right to hold land, depended on grants from the Crown or from some lord: no one, without such authority, might buy or sell or make things for sale in each place, and to have such a right meant being able to prevent others from encroaching on it. The great difference between economic rights in the town and those in the country was that the grants of charters to townsmen were made not to individuals, but to groups. In the towns authority was exercised by corporations; we still call the governing body of a borough 'the corporation'; and within the towns there were other corporations holding property and making rules for the conduct of their members in their business affairs, which we usually call guilds. Besides the corporate guilds, there were others, not in the legal sense corporations, which acted in similar ways, but had their property held for them by the municipal corporation and were more or less under its authority. Co-operation was the characteristic of the organization of the towns, not only because it is easier to co-operate in the close proximity of a town than in the dispersed life of the countryside, but also because, in order to get as good a living as possible, the townsmen wanted to be strong enough to stand up against the wealth and power of surrounding landowners. Like the peasants, they worked each for his own individual profit, but in order to do this they submitted themselves to a system of discipline and mutual aid, sharing, within limits, burdens and advantages, and trying to spread their risks, especially the risk of going short.

The regulations made by these guilds and companies, and also those sometimes made over their heads by the law of the land, were what they were because, in the first place, they were made for a world in which scarcity was never far away and abundance was precarious, intermittent and often disturbing if not disastrous to the trader. When goods are scarce, unless something is done to prevent them, the sellers will ask exorbitant prices and the buyers, whether they buy the goods to consume or to work them up as materials by manufacture, will not all have an equal chance of getting as much as they want. To counteract shortage the guilds made many rules, of a type familiar in many other times and places. They acquired the privilege of preventing everyone from selling except in the open market. Forestalling was prohibited— that is, buying goods before they have been brought to market, and so getting them cheap when buyers in the market may have to buy dearer. Regrating also was forbidden—that is, buying goods in a market and selling them again, of course for a higher price, in or near the same place; and engrossing, buying up goods so as to curtail the supply and raise the price above the former competitive level. The guilds regulated the quality of the wares which their members might make, and this, like some of the other rules, sounds as if it was meant in the interests of the consumer. But it was also in the seller's interest: it prevented price-cutting competition by preventing production at lower cost. The fundamental idea was that there was a certain amount of trade to go round, and it must be shared out fairly between the privileged traders. Competition between them was limited. No one might become a member of the guild unless he had served a long apprenticeship. No master might employ more than a fixed number of apprentices and journeymen, and this not only restricted entry into the guild, but also limited the scale of each business. There were other rules which prevented a master from increasing his output and so lowering his costs and underselling his fellows: in some crafts, for instance, it was forbidden to work by artificial light. This restriction of output was tolerable to the guildsmen because they had their privileged position: they were monopolists and could keep up their prices to the public and keep down the prices at which they bought their raw materials. It was tolerable to the consumers because it was almost entirely local, and both buyers and sellers were neighbours who knew one another's affairs and jealously watched for any attempt at cheating.

In its nature, however, this system restricted output and movement, and two forces were pressing against it, the desire of the consumer to have more goods and have them cheaper, the desire of the seller to sell more goods and make a better living. Thus, in spite of rules against depleting the local supplies of corn, middlemen carried it away from districts where stocks were available to others where they were so badly needed that famine prices could be had. In spite of the right of the local weavers to be the sole sellers of cloth in the market-town, from time to time cloth from distant parts of the country or from overseas was to be had in some fair where bigger traders had gained an overriding privilege to sell. The barriers were weakened, but they were weakened mainly by the assaults of the richer and more powerful sellers. These upset the balance of the little interlocking monopolies. They broke down, for instance, the strict demarcation between separate crafts. By 1496 these processes had gone so far that, just as there were two systems side by side in agriculture, the feudal system and the money system, so in commerce and industry also there were two systems side by side, the corporative system and the competitive system.

Circumstances kept some occupations outside the restrictive system, for instance, the building industry.

For such a sparse and poor population, this was very large and its buildings were made with marvellous craftsmanship and design. The perpendicular style of architecture was entering on its final triumphant stage: the chapel of King's College, Cambridge, was still unfinished; rich men in the wool business were putting up costly parish churches like those of Fairford in Gloucestershire and Long Melford in Suffolk. Stone was little used for houses except for their foundations and lower stories; bricks, either imported from the Low Countries or home-made were used for important buildings, especially in the East, where stone was scarce. The country had an equipment of stone buildings which had to be kept in repair; in England and Wales there were nearly 200 castles, still not regarded as obsolete for defence, many walled towns, thousands of churches, monasteries, hospitals, hundreds of bridges. Rich men devoted large sums to building. Their religious belief gave them a motive for this and they valued beautiful things; but they built the more lavishly because there were few other ways in which they could spend their accumulated wealth. The typical ostentation of the time lay in keeping a great household of servants and other retainers, but that generally involved building too. Building therefore occupied a large labour force, with specialized craftsmen, such as masons, glass-painters, and metal-workers. It was too highly skilled to be managed on the system of feudal labour service, and its work was largely outside the towns, the crafts-men wandering from job to job. Thus masons' guilds were rare; apprenticeship was by no means universal; most of the craftsmen were mere wage-earners, paid for working on raw materials owned by the employers and with very little prospect of rising above that condition. Some of them improved their status by being hired for a full year or even for life. Some had agricultural holdings or other by-occupations for slack times, such as letting houses or carts, shipowning, brewing, inn-keeping, stone-dealing or quarry-owning. The largest employers, like the king or the cathedrals, had well-developed systems of accounting and of managing labour: in the building industry there was a type of man scarcely found as yet in the ordinary urban crafts, the organizer.

Similar results were produced wherever the scale of business transactions was exceptionally large, and this was the case above all where seaborne commerce played a part. The merchant trading with the Continent could bring to bear at one time and place the force of a greater demand and a greater supply than the home trade could concentrate in any sphere except building and the corn trade. English economy was therefore partly moulded by the needs and the capacities of other countries, especially those in Europe.

The continent of Europe, as defined by geographers, has never corresponded with any economic unit. On the east it is separated from Asia by a line which the map-makers have drawn, not always in the same place and never along any natural economic barrier. On the south Europe is bounded by the Mediterranean, and the Mediterranean is a highway. In the last years of the fifteenth century, however, there was very little traffic between Europe and the other continents. There was none of great economic importance except what came in by the two gateways of Portugal and the Levant. The Ottoman Empire was not, as used to be supposed, averse from trading with Christendom, but the Turkish part of it had no manufactured goods to offer. The cargoes which Italian merchants brought home from the ports of the Levant consisted, apart from currants, silken and cotton textiles and Cretan wine, chiefly of the spices, perfumes and drugs of Arabia and the further East. Portugal, the maritime and commercial state of the Atlantic coast, had become the mistress of European trade with West Africa. The Portuguese traded along the coast, bringing home gold, slaves, ivory, pepper, gums and cotton cloth in a very profitable exchange for their wheat, cloths, and horses. They brought sugar and wine from the Atlantic islands. Their trade was expanding every year as they extended their geographical explorations; but it was controlled by royal monopolies, which limited output in order to keep up prices. There was indeed some direct British trade to the Mediterranean and the Levant, and Bristol ships sailed to the Atlantic islands; but in quantity these trades were small. The Atlantic states other than Portugal were indeed beginning to form hopes of oceanic trade. Columbus had discovered the West Indies for Castile. The Pope had divided the New Worlds between Spain and Portugal. King Henry VII did not recognize the validity of this division, and in this year 1496 he gave his patronage to John Cabot for the voyage on which he discovered Newfoundland. But England still depended, for goods from the other continents, on the foreigners who travelled by Portugal and the Levant.

Except for these two streams of commerce, Europe almost formed a closed economic unit. No other part of the civilized world depended on Europe for its luxuries or its necessities; nor indeed was Europe dependent on the rest of the world except for costly imports which added to the enjoyments of the wealthy or the splendours of the Church. Within the European area trade was active and varied. There were great diversities of products and manufactures; regions exceptionally well-placed for producing some commodities were short of others and so sought them by exchange. Europe had better natural opportunities for transport than any equal area of the known world. Two inland seas, the Baltic and the Mediterranean, ran right into it from west to east, the one into a country of cornfields and forests, the other into the warm lands of vines and olives. Both these and the Atlantic had indented coast-lines, deep gulfs, estuaries and long, navigable rivers. Thus the regions were specialized: some produced raw materials which in others, hundreds of miles away, were worked up into textiles, weapons, armour, cutlery, and many other highly finished products, for sale in the remotest corners of Europe. Within Europe there was a complicated interdependence, one region needing the commerce of another for its own prosperity or, in some instances, even for bare subsistence.

England's place in this interdependence was dictated by her natural resources. First there was her mineral wealth. The Cornish tin-mines were the largest source of tin in Europe. Cornwall and part of Devon formed an industrial district, where population was relatively dense, serving a metropolitan and even an international market. The industry was controlled by the royal duchy of Cornwall, and most of the tin went to market in London. There the pewter manufacture had its headquarters. Some pewter vessels were exported; the Pewterers' Company had rights of regulation all

ver England and had to contend with some provincial
alousy. Raw tin was an important export: perhaps
1,000 worth would be shipped abroad in a good year.
fter tin, lead, used mainly as a roofing material, was
f some importance: it came from the Mendips, from
umberland, Yorkshire, Durham and Derbyshire.
mall quantities of coal were shipped across the North
ea from Newcastle, but coal was not used in industry,
nd it was hardly known away from the coalfields,
ough it was worked in all of these except the deep
eams of Kent. Iron was dug by small-holding miners
r little co-operative partnerships in the Forest of
)ean, and the Wealden iron industry in Surrey, Kent
nd Sussex was making increasing quantities of horse-
hoes, nails and utensils. There were smelting works
t Birmingham and in the Clee Hills. Others at
heffield and Rotherham supplied small workshops
here cutlery was made for sale rather in the surround-
ag regions than in the country as a whole. But iron
vas an import, not an export: both Spain and the
ederation of North German trading cities called the
Ianse supplied it. In the same way, the mineral salt of
heshire was supplemented by imported 'bay-salt' from
oitou and further. English mines had nowhere grown
o large as to create communities of an urban character.
The mineral industries except tin and lead were
hus only of domestic importance. The one commodity
vhich linked England closely to the Continent was
vool. England was a great wool-producing country.
Jot only were there many sheep on the grass of the
vide chalk downs; but it was a common calculation
hat in the arable lands every acre of fallow ought to
upport at least two sheep. Opposite England, in the
.ow Countries, was the greatest industrial region of

B

Europe, the cloth-manufacturing region where Bruges, Ghent, Ypres, Tournay, Cambrai, Arras and a score of other towns made the finest textiles for most of the Continent. The English sheep therefore supplied in value perhaps four-fifths of the whole of the export of the country, and the Netherlands predominated greatly over all other countries in English foreign trade.

Medieval foreign trade, like domestic trade, was normally in the hands of privileged companies, though these companies too did not trade on their own account but simply regulated the trade of individual merchants or partnerships. For two reasons, these companies normally conducted their business in fixed places called 'staples'. It suited the governments that they should do so, because they were better able to raise taxes from the trade if they knew where to find it and in whose hands. It suited the merchants because, or rather if they could find at the staple, usually at stated fairs, sufficient buyers to take off all their wares at a good price. Here again a limited quantity was easier to handle profitably than an unlimited quantity. The export of raw wool and wool-fells or fleeces from England was in the hands of a company called the Merchants of the Staple, seated at Calais, the king's one Continental possession, a good gateway to the Low Countries and to the linen-manufacturing district of Northern France. The same company also had the monopoly of exporting tin, lead, hides, butter, and cheese. Another company, the Merchant Adventurers, exported unfinished and undyed cloth through Antwerp. There was no export of finished cloth. About a fifth of the cloth exports were handled by the Hanseatic League at its trading station, called the Steelyard, in London. The Hanse aimed at keeping the whole trade of the Baltic under its control, and the English were not satisfied with this state of things; but by a treaty made at Utrecht in 1474, they had to acquiesce in it. In 1491, however, King Henry had obtained a grant for his subjects of a partial right to trade in Danzig. Commercial treaties were an exceptional method of regulating international intercourse. Usually a prince merely granted to foreigners, without corresponding concessions on their side of the water, the privilege of trading without vexation in his dominions. It is therefore significant that English relations with the Netherlands were regulated by an elaborate treaty of the year 1478, which embodied clauses from a number of earlier agreements.

The treaty is significant of the fact, which both parties understood, that the interdependence of England and the Netherlands was mutual: neither could do without the other. Economically, however, it was of a kind which, on an infinite number of occasions in history, has appeared to one of the two parties to operate unfairly in favour of the other. England was the new country, relatively undeveloped, selling a raw or partly finished product to the richer manufacturing country. The Netherlands owed their great wealth to the profits of their dyeing, finishing, and high-grade weaving. Their business knowledge and connexions seemed to make it impossible for the English to set up remunerative manufactures of their own or to raise the selling price of wool. It is true that this was not a simple or extreme case of a primary producer tied to a manufacturing country. The Netherlands could buy some wool from Spain, and in a small way England was to two still poorer countries what the Netherlands were to her. In Ireland she had a small and dilapidated colony, consisting of four counties and a number of seaports, with a primitive and hostile country beyond. She sold cloth, salt, iron and manufactured articles to Ireland in exchange for hides, wool, linen, linen yarn, and cheap rough cloth. In Bergen, the staple for all foreign trade in Norway, she had a similar position. But Scandinavian trade was very small. There was no direct trade with Sweden. In other directions there were no promising alternative outlets for wool which might have made the Netherlands less able to trade in England on their own terms. In France, indeed, Normandy, Picardy and Champagne were buyers, but not on a large scale. In the Mediterranean Venice maintained a strong protectionist policy of staple trade in Western and Eastern products. The Venetian State fleets touched annually at Southampton on their Flanders voyage, but King Henry wanted to free English trade from Venetian control. In 1490 he had made a treaty with the rival republic of Florence for the export of wool and for the protection of English shipping; but this and other measures of his had led to Venetian counter-measures and then to English retaliation which in the end left trade no better off.

In this economic nationalism, which was supported by a number of merchants and others, the English had some advantages. The country was politically unified, with a strong monarchy as monarchies were then, and so in negotiation it could take advantage of rivalries between the Italian states, disagreements among the Hanseatic towns and conflicts of interest between the different towns and provinces of the Netherlands. But its bargaining position was not strong. It could not exert pressure on any of the great commercial states by refusing to buy their wares, for England was not a very great buyer of any class of goods. Its imports were a miscellaneous list, some materials, like woad from France and Germany, and alum from Italy, which it needed for cloth-making and dyeing, then wine, fish, salt, Eastern spices, fine textiles. Above all, it was hard to get a footing in the overseas markets for cloth. The human race has usually been better off for clothing than for food. The textile industries usually grow in advance of all others: both the raw material and the finished products are durable, and the means of producing them are easily expanded. In the later fifteenth century the established industrial districts were making more cloth than they could easily dispose of; English economic nationalism had to face protectionist opposition everywhere.

The woollen manufacture in England had developed out of all proportion to other industries. There were well-defined industrial districts. About half the woollens were made in the west—that is, in Gloucestershire, Wiltshire, Somerset, with outlying districts in Oxfordshire, Berkshire, Hampshire, Dorset, Devon, and Cornwall. The best broadcloth for export came from Wiltshire. Another quarter of the woollens came from East Anglia. Here a branch of the industry, named from the Norfolk village of Worsted, had its chief home: it used long-fibred wool and made a durable stuff, not felted like the woollens, but apt to become shiny with use. The West Riding of Yorkshire was another rising centre of manufactures, which spread up the dales as far as Kendal in Westmorland. Towards the Welsh border the dyers and finishers of Shrewsbury handled the coarse Welsh woollens, and there was a considerable manufacture in Gloucester,

Worcester, and other towns. Coventry was the great place for caps. There was competition between different places; some were thriving and others decaying.

The organization of the industry was far from uniform; but in many places the pull of the distant markets had brought in large-scale operations and an elaborate division of functions. The simple local craftsman who sold by retail had his loom and shop and dwelling-place all in one. He owned them all and bought materials outside. Though he might be indebted to the sellers or other creditors, he was the sole master of his apprentices and journeymen. The merchants of London or Bristol or Southampton wanted to deal with a different kind of man, someone who could supply larger quantities, of reliable quality and by fixed dates. When the producer no longer dealt with the consumer, at some point or other in the chain of buying and selling a man would set up as a dealer. With his profits he was able to establish control over the masters in the manufacturing processes. This he did, not by owning the workshops, but by owning the materials. Under this system the large-scale industry grew up alongside of the small-scale: John Tame of Fairford, who was living at this time, owning sheep, dealing in wool, making cloth, became the lord of several manors. Thomas Spring, of Lavenham in Suffolk, married his daughter to a son of the Earl of Oxford.

These clothiers grew great by the 'putting-out' system. There was nothing new in the system itself. Caxton, in his translation of *The Golden Legend*, writes that the mother of St. Edmund Rich, Mabel the Rich of Abingdon, who lived in the thirteenth century, 'put out wool for to spin'. The clothier bought wool from the graziers, put it out to be spun by cottagers and others, collected the yarn from them and put it out again to weavers who made it into cloth to his specification. The wool, the yarn, and the cloth were his; the spinners and weavers, though they owned their own distaffs or spinning-wheels or looms, worked for piece-work wages. This system may be described in terms more or less complimentary to the capitalistic traders. When an independent weaver could not sell his cloth and so could not pay for yarn he might have no choice but to sacrifice his independence by working the clothier's yarn for wages. He sold himself for bread in the evil days; but, on the other hand, he might gain steady employment, for the clothier, with his warehouse and his strings of packhorses, could sell at favourable times or in chosen markets. He did not need to carry a finished piece on his back to the nearest town and to bring back the price, however low it might be, to buy more yarn or to buy the next month's food. If the weaver had a little farm, as many of them had, he was insured against unemployment and temporary depressions of prices, so the transition to the putting-out system was slow. And except in textiles it had scarcely made its appearance.

From the employer's point of view, the putting-out system had disadvantages. It cost much time in fetching and carrying; it gave the worker opportunities for stealing from the material entrusted to him. But the only industrial establishments at this time where there was anything like the discipline and concentration of factory labour were in trades where work could not be done at all unless someone stood the expense of owning and equipping a large productive unit.

Ship-building was one of these, and there were coming to be more. There were a good many machines in use which cost more money to make and run than a loom or a lathe. There were corn mills, fulling mills, cutler mills, pumps in the Cornish mines; in this year 1496 we hear of a tilt-hammer; and to all these water, wind or horse-power was applied. There were blast furnaces and cranes. Although they were very small these all needed money behind them, so there was a connexion between capitalism and technological development. There were some new industries which had recently been introduced by moneyed men. The manufacture of gunpowder was one. The most interesting had to do with book-production, though we may note in passing that by 1496 no book of economic interest had yet been printed in England. It was in that year that the first book printed on English-made paper came out.

Most of the new tendencies to expansion and to the concentration of wealth and economic power were stronger in London than anywhere else in the kingdom. London had by far the greatest share of English overseas trade, and we have seen how London had a hand in the great businesses of wool and corn and tin. Close by, at Westminster, was the seat of government, and London and Lisbon were the only western capitals which were also great ports. Each of the major occupations supported a crowd of ancillary craftsmen. down the river were shipwrights and rope-makers; the lawyers needed parchment; everyone patronized brewers, tailors, and leather-sellers; there were hundreds of innkeepers and vintners. When King Henry VII entered London in 1485 he was met by

435 guildsmen riding on horseback in gowns of bright mulberry colour and representing sixty-five 'mysteries'. The local government of the City was based on the election of civic officers by the guildsmen and no one but a guildsman might drive any trade there; but in London the guild constitution was not merely restrictive and conservative. To begin with, there was the 'custom of London' according to which a citizen duly qualified for membership in any one of the companies might carry on, not merely the business proper to that company, but any other, at least in buying and selling, though perhaps not in manufacture. Thus a man could change his trade, and, which was more important, he could build up his business by buying control over workers in other crafts. There were many business men in London who described themselves in official documents by the old guild names, but who were in fact merchant capitalists buying and selling many kinds of goods in distant markets. Some of them travelled to and fro between London and the Low Countries or Calais; but others were fixed in their London counting-houses or were members of firms which had one or more partners always there when one went overseas.

These higher traders and the other substantial men whose trade was in England had their own grip on the guild system. In recent years a number of the London companies had obtained charters of incorporation from the Crown, the terms of which distinguished them in three ways from the rest. They amalgamated together various crafts which had been separately organized; they placed the new company under the control of an oligarchic governing body, recruited, not by election, but by co-optation, and so they left the way open for separate organizations of the 'yeomanry', the lesser masters who remained outside the governing body. The City, at first jealous of the power given by the Crown to these 'livery companies', had itself adopted the practice of granting a similar organization to others, so that about half the city crafts were organized in this way. A similar tendency on a smaller scale was at work in some of the provincial towns. The increase and concentration of wealth thus created a number of antagonisms, which strained and shifted the balance of economic power. There was the antagonism between the Londoners and the provincial business men; there was the antagonism between the liveries and the yeomanry. Another antagonism was that between the City on the one hand and on the other the suburbs and the 'liberties' within the city boundaries, where, for one reason or another, the civic authorities had no jurisdiction. A man debarred from the privilege of working or trading in the City might set up as a competitor in one of these, and many did so, especially foreigners, such as the weavers, of whom there were considerable numbers in Southwark.

Business methods of all kinds were naturally more advanced in London than elsewhere. Some of the greatest businesses of the time were one-man businesses; but partnership was a familiar way of joining together the resources of several men. The law laid down many rules for partnerships. A partnership was an agreement between individuals: it had to be renewed whenever one of them for any reason ceased to be a partner. No partner could transfer his share to anyone else. The share of the profits which each partner was to take was one of the matters defined by the agreement. The financial organization of the foreign trade was far from primitive. Bills of exchange were the normal means of payment, and the trade in bills—in other words, the credit system—employed a number of specialized operators. It does not seem, however, that there were more than a few, if any, English business men who handled only money and not goods as well. Nor, even amongst these, was accountancy up to the level which the Italian and Flemish merchants had reached. We do not know of any Englishman who kept a double-entry ledger as early as this date, and no book on this system had yet been printed in English. According to canon law, all persons exercising merchandise had to pay to the Church personal tithes on the 'clear gain' of their business. They paid yearly; but it appears that they had no exact means of calculating their net profits, and the tithe-owners made bargains with them, probably on the basis of the annual value of the premises they occupied.

The economic life of the towns, even of London, was simple, and its scale was small. One of the greatest figures in English trade a few years before this time was William Cannynges, the great benefactor of St. Mary Redcliffe Church, who owned nearly half the shipping of Bristol. We are told of him that he had ten ships, totalling 2,930 tons, with 800 seamen, and that he employed a hundred masons, carpenters, and artificers. It is true that at all times the wealth invested and the numbers employed in shipping are small in proportion to its economic importance; but these figures show how primitive England still was. The great man's fleet could carry less than one small tramp steamer of the present day, and if we remember the slowness and uncertainty of the voyages and the short distances for which victuals could be carried without replenishing, the discrepancy is greater still. Again, although the number of men may well be much exaggerated, it reminds us that for every ton of shipping afloat, as for every piece on the looms and every bushel of wheat from the fields, far more labour was needed in those days of simple tools and equipment than now. The output of goods per head was comparable with that of the simpler Asiatic societies of our day.

Conscious planning played a very modest part in the economy of this time. In the main the Church, the king and his servants, the municipalities, or the guilds used their limited power of social control, not to impose economic plans, but merely to prevent breaches of traditional rules and standards, or at most to adapt these standards to the exigencies of changing situations. There was a certain stock of economic ideas. They were good ideas, though they were simple and general, and the written discussions of them were not to any serious extent analytical, but intended only to clarify them and apply them to the relatively complex facts of economic life. Like most systematic thought at that time, these ideas were a branch of a comprehensive interpretation of the whole universe. The Church was the custodian of this interpretation, although laymen wrote pamphlets on commercial policy.

The main doctrines had to do with economic justice, the principles of fair dealing. There was the doctrine that in all transactions a just price ought to be paid. This might be explained so as to mean very little more than that a seller committed a sin if he took more than the correct price, the market price; but it was often explained so as to condemn something more than simple cheating. If it penetrated a little into economic analysis, it meant that the market price itself ought to be just, and that meant, roughly speaking, that it ought to depend on the cost of production and not on unfair competition or on the power of a monopolist. There was one special sphere in which the doctrine of just price took a form very natural in a peasant society: in the sphere of finance it took the form of condemning usury. There were texts in Scripture and in Aristotle which seemed to mean that all loans should be without interest; and this was the official theory. Even in this peasant society, where no one needed to borrow except in misfortune, this official theory did not prevent the rise of the usurious lender and his counterpart, the improvident borrower; but in the world of business and money economy there were many provident borrowers and many indispensable lenders. Theoretically what we call 'credit' was usury, one example of the sin of avarice; but the theologians and lawyers admitted many exceptions to the theory, so that credit might be given legitimately wherever the honest creditor would have suffered loss if no interest was paid. Avarice in all its forms was to be seen everywhere; but it was much more commonly censured than improvidence or idleness. There were indeed long-standing laws to put down begging by any who were able to work, especially those who had got adrift from the townships where they were born; but charity was universally recognized as a duty. Although the poverty of some of the religious orders had become so formal as to be scarcely distinguishable from wealth, it was the general opinion that a poor beggar might be better off than the rich man who made a bad use of the wealth entrusted to him.

Ideas like these, taking much for granted and, however minutely the schoolmen worked them out, leaving many questions unasked, were enough for most people; but those who had the government of the country in their hands had to consider further problems. Their first concerns were to protect their own power against rivals and to prevent disputes which might threaten the peace. This led them to assume a certain general control of economic associations. They did not use these powers to impose an economic policy on the guilds. Their action in general was quite unlike that of modern governments in times of shortage, for the simple reason that the machinery of the State was still weak and incapable of undertaking any but simple tasks. Anything like rationing, for instance, was utterly impossible, and the law of the land put no effective restraint on the freedom of the individual to buy whatever he could afford. There was a sumptuary law or Act of Apparel on the Statute Book, prohibiting the use of expensive and luxurious materials except by people qualified in an ascending scale by rank and wealth. It was not, however, enforced, and the only enactment of Henry VII on apparel told in the opposite direction: it fixed maximum prices for hats and caps. There was no statutory regulation of what people might eat or what sort of houses they might live in. The only effective restraint on consumption was that of the ecclesiastical rules for fasting.

Henry VII was a very successful ruler, and one of the chief reasons for his success was that he was a financier. He had begun his reign with debts, but by this time his finances were sound; he had annual surpluses and he was building up a considerable 'treasure' in the form of plate and jewels. It is not clear how much he improved on the administrative practice of his predecessors, but it is certain that he worked hard at finance himself and that he made money in a variety of ways. In 1492 he had made the King of France promise him annual payments which in about fifteen years were to bring in £159,000: they amounted to a good deal more than double his land revenue in each year. When he had extraordinary expenditure for military preparations or the like, it was paid for by parliamentary taxes. Of these the most usual were tenths and fifteenths, taxes which had originally been meant as levies of these fractions on different kinds of property. They were apportioned taxes—that is to say that each county had to raise a sum assigned to it by allotting the burden in its turn on the payers. The total amount had not been charged for more than a century. The machinery for levying these taxes was obsolete and ineffective. Special taxes were levelled on aliens, and the clergy taxed themselves in Convocation.

Henry's first Parliament also granted him the Customs for life, and his revenue from these taxes on foreign trade was more than £30,000 a year in the first ten years of his reign and more than £40,000 in the remainder. This increase was probably due partly to good management; but, in working up his Customs revenue, Henry mainly relied on increasing trade. We have seen that he backed up the English merchants in their disputes in the Low Countries and in their contests with the Venetians and the Hanse. He adopted a protectionist policy, because protection was what the trading companies asked for. His protectionist measures were tentative and experimental; they were not strictly enforced; but when one came off another went on, and we may say that at this time the State acted on two ideas in relation to foreign trade. In the first place, it encouraged imports and exports in order to be able to tax them. In the second place, the State tried to get as much of the trade as possible into the hands of its own subjects. This was done, not by a protective tariff, but by the direct manipulation of privileged rights to trade in this or that commodity at this or that place. It was protectionism of a territorial rather than an economic kind: the State decided, not what transactions should take place, but what persons should carry them out. A special case was the control of the movements of coin and the precious metals. There was a certain amount of established monetary theory, and it was agreed that the realm would be impoverished if its money ran short. The law therefore supplemented the king's monopoly of coinage by making it a felony to carry out of the kingdom without licence any English coin, or any plate, bullion or jewels of gold or silver. It was a penal offence to melt down coin, and all alien merchants were to spend the money received for their merchandise on commodities of the realm. This law, like the others, could be evaded; but, taken together, they forced trade into approved channels and so restricted it. On the other hand, foreign trade remained much more free than home trade. There were no fixed prices; there was no limit to the numbers the merchants might employ or the branches of trade they might engage in. Foreign trade already had the men and the financial technique best adapted for expansion. It was small in volume, and it handled only a small part of the nation's production; but in the year of John Cabot's expedition it was looking for opportunities.

CHAPTER II

ENGLAND DURING THE PRICE REVOLUTION, TO 1572

LET us move forward and compare the country we have just described with England as it was fourteen years after the accession of Queen Elizabeth, in 1572, the year of the Massacre of St. Bartholomew, the year in which the Dutch broke out in revolt against the Duke of Alva. The first changes to notice are changes in the geography of the realm. Calais had been lost. For a short time this Continental bridgehead had been extended by the capture of Boulogne, but now both were gone, and England had no possession of her own in which to set up a Continental staple. Wales had been incorporated with England. One result of this was that the peasants of Wales now had landlords of the English type; and though there was little change in the economic life of this poor and sequestered region, there was better order, and somewhat more intercourse with England, an improvement, so far as it went, in England's economic position, as well as in that of Wales.

At this time the population of England and Wales can be estimated more clearly than at the earlier date: it was probably somewhat above four millions. Whether this means that it had increased we cannot be certain; but, if it had, the increase was moderate and we can say little about its causes. There had been both immigration and emigration and both were still in progress: immigration to the busy east and southeast from the industrial districts of the Continent, emigration to Ireland. The English foothold in Ireland had been strengthened both by renewed military and administrative energy and by a new policy of colonization: Philip and Mary had 'planted' King's County and Queen's County.

These movements of migration made no large, direct change in the numbers of the English population: they ran into tens of thousands but not into hundreds of thousands. Their importance is that they show, on the one hand, industrial districts prospering so as to be able to absorb new hands; on the other, a surplus of adventurous men either dissatisfied with their lot or at least willing to take their chance of improving it overseas. The reason why we know more about these matters in the sixteenth century than in the fifteenth is that administrators now had them recorded more exactly. This was partly because the stresses of the times called for stricter government: many of the alien immigrants were religious refugees, at once welcome and suspect from the 'ideological' point of view. They had to be organized as communities; suitable spheres of work had to be marked out for them side by side with the existing guilds, and so records of their numbers were kept. But there was another motive for keeping records of the people. Governments wanted to know more in order to be able to do more. This is exemplified by the institution of parish registers. Some parish priests had kept registers of christenings, marriages and burials for their own purposes: it was as well to know who were already married and who were within the prohibited degrees. These records seem to have been made compulsory first in Spain; the practice passed to the Spanish Netherlands and thence in 1538 Thomas Cromwell introduced it here. Perhaps his purpose was to tax the sacraments; at any ate, Parliament tried to do so in 1563. Whatever his purpose may have been, he provided modern historians with some rudimentary information from which to construct vital statistics.

In the distribution of population there had been one change which was symptomatic of everything we know about the Tudor period: London had grown. We do not know how much it had grown, but one estimate is that the City and suburbs together now had more than 100,000 inhabitants. It had grown more quickly than the population of the country as a whole. A greater proportion of the nation's business was now done in London; and this probably means that a greater proportion, and a greater absolute amount, of the nation's capital and labour was now devoted to the kinds of business that were done there. London's proportionate share in the receipts of the Customs had increased considerably. It would be rash to infer too much from this fact, since we cannot calculate how much of it merely reflects changes in the tariff or in the efficiency of collection; but London certainly was becoming more of an economic metropolis. We shall see later that there were changes, difficult to analyse, in the distribution of the provincial population, and we may suppose that people were moving into London from rural areas. Whether the other towns were growing much it is hard to say. Some of the fishing and trading ports were busy and probably growing, but others were decayed; some of the clothing towns had recently suffered from the competition of rural industries. Perhaps the gains slightly exceeded the losses.

The greatest change in the face of the country was made by the enclosures of open fields, but we must defer our discussion of these until we have mentioned some other changes. Apart from the cultivated land, the fixed capital or durable economic equipment of the country seems on the whole to have been improved, though there were some setbacks and nothing was changed out of recognition. In the draining of marshes there seems to have been no great activity, and some ground was even lost. In 1532 a great general Act of Parliament laid down the duties and powers of the 'Commissioners of sewers' who were to have charge of drainage works up and down the country; but only private enterprise could undertake large schemes of reclamation. In Somerset the abbots of Glastonbury had reclaimed land in the old days, but, after the dissolution of their monastery, Meare Poole was spreading, and it got worse until the late eighteenth century. In Queen Elizabeth's time an Italian engineer, Jacobus Acontius, with his partners, made some progress towards recovering 2,000 acres of land which had been inundated by the sea in the parishes of Erith, Lessness, and Plumstead, towards the Thames Estuary. On the whole it seems that there was less activity of this kind than in the previous period; and this may be due to either of two causes. Possibly investment in gaining land was now less remunerative over the country generally in comparison with investment in trade or manufacture and, as we shall see, there was much more ready-made land in the market; but the reason may in some instances be less interesting: it may only be that there were fewer men with the necessary funds and energy in the localities where drainage could be undertaken. The abbots had gone, and, as we shall see, some of the lay landowners were financially embarrassed.

The most notable new works of civil engineering

had to do with transport. A series of Acts of Parliament, especially in the time of Henry VIII, pressed on the work of removing obstructions from rivers and clearing them where they had silted up. The first pound-locks in England were built in about 1564 on the canal at Exeter. Partly for naval reasons, which were closely allied with those of commerce when sea warfare was mainly carried on by hired merchant ships, the Tudors and their parliaments ordered much work on the ports: £65,000 was spent on Dover pier. Henry VIII gave a charter to the Trinity House on Deptford Strand, and Elizabeth gave it additional powers over beacons and sea-marks. On land the roads, so far as we know, had not changed much for the better; but a step towards national control over their material condition was taken by an Act of Philip and Mary which laid on the parishes the duty of keeping the highways in repair. Money economy had not yet conquered this region: there was no rate to pay, but the landowners had to supply stone, the farmers carts, and the labourers their labour. In the types of vehicles in use there is no great change to notice; but a new kind of traffic, of great importance, had begun. Henry VIII had copied from France a rudimentary postal system. A 'master of the posts' was responsible for royal correspondence on the Berwick and Calais roads and sometimes on the Bristol route to Ireland. Between Gravesend and Dover there were hackney horses for travellers to hire. By 1572 the system had extended considerably. Though ordinary private letters might be carried by anyone, the postmaster at the head of it was also in charge of a private service organized by the merchants for carrying their letters to the Continent.

England was better equipped for movement and intercourse than in the time of Henry VII, and there had been corresponding changes in foreign commerce. The Spaniards and Portuguese had opened up all the coasts of South and Central America, Africa, India, and the Malay Archipelago, and they were bringing great quantities of goods to Europe. It is indeed disputed whether the change from the old trade routes to the oceanic highways had by this time led to any great increase in the volume of goods brought into Europe; but, however this may be, the map of commerce had entirely changed. Not only did western and central Europe now get most of their Asiatic imports by sea carriage round the Cape; the commerce of Europe was now centred as it had never been before in a single port. Antwerp, in the heart of the trading and industrial district of the Netherlands, had become the distributing centre through which a great part of the Continent carried on its long-distance commerce. The Merchant Adventurers had their 'factory', or trading-post, there, principally for the sale of unfinished cloth, and they were now the most important English trading company: the Staplers had lost some of their privileges and much of their trade. The Portuguese had moved their staple for spices to Antwerp from Lisbon. It was the world market for pepper and the greatest European money market. There were other international capitalists in Genoa and Lyons, and the international financial machinery made dealings all over western and central Europe comparatively easy; but Antwerp was its heart. England's close economic connexion with the Low Countries brought her, as we shall see, a share in these advantages; but she was still the dependent neighbour. She had made no breach in the Spanish and Portuguese monopolies of their new worlds. She had no trading stations in the seaports outside Europe, and she had not attempted to settle any colony. After John Cabot there had been an interval of two generations in which Englishmen had taken scarcely any interest in the search for new lands; most of them found in Europe the outlet they needed for their exports. The one direct economic result of Cabot's discovery was that fishermen from the Atlantic coasts of Europe, including some scores or hundreds from the south-west of England, went out every summer to the rich cod-fishing grounds off Newfoundland.

The new period in English exploration did not begin in earnest until the reign of Edward VI, when Sir Hugh Willoughby and Richard Chancellor set out to seek China by the north-east passage, the route round the northern coast of Siberia which was never travelled from end to end until 1879. But when it did begin it was a new period in commerce as well as in navigation. Willoughby and Chancellor failed in their first aim; but their voyage led to the opening up of the first new market for English exports, the Russian market. In 1572 the Russian trade had been suspended for two years, and, apart from that, it had not fulfilled the high hopes with which it began. At first it looked as if the Tsar would allow the new English company trading through Archangel, not only to sell English goods in his dominions, but to be the sole exporters of Russian produce—that is, of whale oil, tallow, furs, felt, and the very profitable commodities cordage, masts, and wax. The Russians, however, captured Narva, a great centre of Hanseatic trade, and began to trade through the Baltic themselves. They also gave up the plan of limiting their favour to a single group of foreign merchants who had, in fact, no corresponding advantages to offer. For one reason and another, the Russian trade had proved unprofitable, but it left a by-product, the trade through Archangel to the Volga and so to the Caspian and Persia. The value of the Oriental goods brought by this route in a good year was perhaps in the region of a thirtieth of the annual shipment of goods by the Merchant Adventurers; but the trade was proportionately more profitable.

Not only had a beginning been made in opening up new markets; a beginning had also been made in a new form of organization, the joint-stock company. Such companies have arisen in different countries at different times with many variations of legal forms and antecedents; the joint-stock principle is a great instrument of economic expansion. A joint-stock company differed from the 'regulated' companies of the Middle Ages: it did not merely organize the trade of its individual members, but itself traded as a corporation. It differed from a partnership in that it went on when individual participants died or left it. Their shares might be sold or inherited and, although this did not come about fully for some time, it is characteristic of the joint-stock company that its shares are marketable. Again, the shareholders took their profits in proportion to the amount of their shares not, as in a partnership, in proportions agreed upon specially in a deed. Thus joint stock suited the investor who was not actively engaged in the business, and from the early days of English joint-stock companies one of their advantages was that they could make the resources of the landowners or the city men in general available for enterprises on a scale too large for any ordinary partnership or firm. By 1572 altogether about £100,000 had been invested in them in London, where they had their headquarters, unlike the old companies, which were seated abroad. Besides the Russia Company and a mining company which will be mentioned later, the trade to Africa had made use of the joint-stock device. In the fifteen-fifties there had been voyages to the west coast, in which Queen Elizabeth participated, on a rudimentary joint-stock principle. Except for this they would not be worth mentioning in an economic history, for they were on a very small scale; and the same may be said of the momentous adventure of Sir John Hawkins, the first English slave-trader, who in 1562 seized 300 negroes and sold them in the West Indies. In 1572 there was no longer any trade with Africa: for the time being this rash enterprise had extinguished the trade by arousing the hostility of Spain.

Now that Englishmen had traded direct to Russia, Persia, Africa, and the West Indies, they thought of freeing themselves from their dependence on the Low Countries. One of them had written in 1550:

This realm hath three commodities, wool, tin and lead,
Which being wrought within the realm each man might get
    his bread.

When he wrote this, in all probability much more of the wool was wrought within the realm than forty years earlier, and by 1572 this was certainly the case. Four-fifths of our exports still came from the sheep's backs; but a greater proportion now went in the form of unfinished cloth, and a smaller proportion as raw wool. To Persia even dyed and finished cloth was sent, though in very small quantities. There was another change, more important at this stage than the rise in cloth exports: the English manufacturing districts were now turning out materials for which we had previously depended on imports from the Low Countries. For the time being these had little or no sale abroad; the home market absorbed them. They were bays, says, and perpetuanas, lighter and finer kinds of cloth than the old English cloths; made by more highly skilled and more highly paid workmen, and therefore requiring more capital to finance the production. Their manufacture had come in gradually from the Continent. We first hear of the 'new draperies' in the early years of Queen Elizabeth. Colchester was the great centre, and the manufacture spread all along the border of Essex and Suffolk.

It is often thought that, since so many of these craftsmen were religious exiles, the new draperies were merely a windfall caused by the Reformation; but it may well be that the same economic process would have happened if England had remained a Catholic country. Textile workers, and even entrepreneurs of considerable wealth had come over before the Reformation. The religious refugees had other countries open to them; they did not hurry over without looking where they were going. England offered them safety and, with the hope of deriving advantage in its turn, it gave them privileges; but it also offered better opportunities for profit than they had in the crowded competitive conditions of the Netherlands or France. There was a market among the population which was growing in numbers and wealth; the chief raw material, wool, was nearer at hand, labour was cheaper; there were, since the Tudors came in, better conditions of law and order. Part of the high-grade Continental textile industry transferred itself to

England, and the fundamental reason was that it moved, as it had moved often enough on the mainland, to the place where capital and management could earn a better remuneration.

About the same time there was another migration of foreign capital and labour into England, of a different character. Queen Elizabeth in her early years made a number of agreements for the mining of various metals. The Crown claimed the right to dispose of all precious metals in the ground, and, though some landowners tried to contest this claim, the law courts upheld it. In the sixteenth century the demand for all sorts of metals was increasing all over Europe, especially because of the increasing use of firearms and munitions of all kinds. For these iron, copper, and lead were needed: gun-metal was an alloy of copper and tin, bullets were made of lead, swords and armour of steel. In mining and metallurgy of all kinds the south German industry was technically the most efficient and financially the most highly developed in Europe. The capitalists of Augsburg and other German centres had already exploited mines all over central Europe, and they had business relations with England in Antwerp, where they sold their wares and where they also took part in the international loan-market. England, the new country, had undeveloped mineral resources, and the English market for metals of all kinds was growing. The first cannon cast in England were made at Buxted in Sussex in about 1543. Early in Elizabeth's reign a partnership, of which two members were Sir Henry Sidney of Penshurst, Sir Philip Sidney's father, and Joan Knight of London, widow, laid out £1,960 on an ironworks in the Weald of Kent. About the same time thirty foreign workmen

came to the ironworks at Robertsbridge. But to ex-
ploit other metals in the remoter parts of England
the greater financial resources of Germany also had
to come into play.

The Queen therefore granted to some German
capitalists, in conjunction with Englishmen, the right
to extract lead and copper and other metals. They
brought over engineers and skilled workmen, Catholics,
and started operations in the Lake District. They
discovered calamine, the ore of zinc, in the Mendips,
and so began the brass industry in England, brass
being a mixture of copper and zinc, which superseded
the old yellow metal, latten, a mixture of copper and
tin.[1] The financial organization of the new metal
industries had several notable features. The Mines
Royal and Battery Company, which was formed both
for mining and for the making of brass-ware or
'battery', was on a joint-stock basis. The Crown did
not want England to become a mere source of supply
for Continental industries, and so the export of the
new metals was prohibited. The main achievement of
the new mining development of this time was in fact
that it provided materials for the industries of Birmingham, Sheffield, and other districts. These were
still organized in small units; the putting-out system
had appeared, but had made little headway.

Besides the new metal industries and the new
draperies, there were other new industries, mostly
working for the home market. The need for munitions led to an increase in the manufacture of gunpowder, and in 1561 a patent was granted for finding
saltpetre, one of its ingredients. Similar grants of

[1] But 'brass' also meant bronze, as in the expression 'a
brass farthing' or the Yorkshireman's 'brass'.

monopoly rights were issued for the use of new, or rather foreign, methods in glass-making and the extraction of sea-salt. Italian methods of making satins and fustians were introduced at Norwich in the time of Philip and Mary, the only craft in this period which obtained privileges by parliamentary authority. In all these grants the Government evidently had one eye on lessening England's dependence on imports. There were some new crafts which owed nothing to privilege. The making of bone lace or pillow lace began in Buckinghamshire before the middle of the century: the tradition that it was brought in from Flanders and by Queen Katharine of Aragon may be untrue, but it seems to fit the right date. The art of knitting by hand appears to have come in about the same time.

Adding together all these new activities, some writers have said that an industrial revolution was in full swing in England from about the time of the dissolution of the monasteries. Some of the new processes could not be carried on except on what was for those days a large scale; they therefore needed comparatively large capital and they tended to employ wage labour. A special point of some interest has been made in connexion with coal. Coal-production was increasing. Perhaps four times as much was produced in 1551–60 as in 1541–50. For the later of the two decades the total is estimated at 210,000 tons from the whole of our island, the north-eastern coalfield and the Midlands each contributing about a quarter and Scotland a fifth. It seems to have been in this period that coal was first used as an industrial fuel. It was used in the new salt and glass industries, and later in a number of others. Now, it happened that much of the coal-bearing land had belonged to monasteries, and though they had allowed their coal to be worked, it is suggested that the lay landowners who succeeded them may have been more willing to allow the output of coal to be increased. They may, for instance, have granted leases for longer terms of years and at easier rents, relying on greater quantities for their compensation. This contention has, however, not been fully proved. Demand may have risen independently and so have promoted the easier supply, and no one can say how the monks would have reacted to it if they had still been there.

It is safe to say that the progress of industrialization was accompanied by a greater zeal for development. There was hardly anything in England yet which could be called technological literature, but there were writers who took notice of invention as a praiseworthy activity. Polydor Vergil, a typical Italian Renaissance scholar, who visited England for the first time in 1502–15, had published in 1499 a famous book 'on the inventors of things' which drew attention to the new devices which were being multiplied every day. The first Italian book on bookkeeping by double entry had appeared in 1496, the work of a friar who was a friend of Leonardo da Vinci. It found its way to England in a curious way: it was translated from Italian into Dutch, from Dutch into French, and from French into an English version which was published in 1547. By 1572 other such books had appeared and the practice was becoming acclimatized. Another symptom of the innovating movement in economic life was the appearance of 'technological unemployment'. In 1552 Parliament prohibited the use of gig-mills, a new mechanical device for raising the nap on cloth, which was depriving old-fashioned hand-workers of their livelihood. For the time being this Act was unique. The other inventions of the period had not attracted the attention of Parliament. England was still a comparatively backward country. If we had statistics, we should probably find that the new ventures added little to the total production of the country. If they reduced the quantity of imports, they made it easier to pay for the other imports from abroad for which no home-made substitute could be found, such as wine, which accounted for a third of the imports from France, and, most important of all, money, which, as we shall see, had to be borrowed at expensive rates in Antwerp. But in reckoning the advantage derived from the new industries, we have to deduct the loss of imports from the gain in home production: if the net wealth of the country—that is, the amount consumed together with the amount added to capital—increased, it had not increased very much by 1572. At that date the advance in industrialization had not made the country very much richer. It had brought in new devices in technology and finance, but on a small scale, so that they were important rather for what they promised than for what they yielded. The England of 1572 was probably more productive than the England of 1496; it was certainly somewhat better equipped for production, and it was finding ways of equipping itself still better.

Moralists indeed lamented, as they usually do, that luxury was on the increase. It seems certain that many men had more comforts than their grandfathers. Farmers used stuffed pillows instead of blocks of wood; they wore nightshirts instead of being content to keep on their day clothes. It would be hard to say whether the rise in the standard of living was general; it certainly was not universal. There were new kinds of maladjustment and the most noticeable novelty in the England of 1572 was acute and widespread economic discontent. There was an extensive printed literature setting out the grievances of the poor and oppressed even when it condemned their violent attempts at a remedy. The printing presses had been pouring out such matter for two generations. Except for a masterpiece like More's *Utopia* (of 1516), the earlier pieces and the immediate occasions that provoked them were forgotten; but it was known to everyone that there was a social problem. It was indeed deliberately brought home by Government propaganda. The churchwardens of every parish had to buy the *Book of Homilies*. In the new editions from 1571 there was a sermon against wilful rebellion, with denunciations of the popular risings of previous years; but the older parts of the book were still in use, and there it was written that, as we say now, there was poverty in the midst of plenty: 'In abundance and plenty of all things we yet complain of want and penury.'

CHAPTER III

FORCES OF CHANGE, TO 1572

THIS state of things had been brought about by great interconnected changes which no one foresaw in 1496. These changes liberated and intensified the two innovating tendencies already at work, mercantile enterprise and the growth of money economy. The first of them, one which originated outside England, was the price revolution. From about the middle of the sixteenth century, English people, especially poor people, began to complain that things were getting dearer, and these complaints went on and grew louder from then until the time we are speaking of. Food was costing more. The sharpest rise of all was in the prices of cattle and horses. In the sixteenth century agricultural prices were always, as the prices of industrial raw materials, especially metals, are now, the most sensitive to economic change. For about twenty years the politicians and the writers who offered remedies for the social problem were puzzled. This was unlike the familiar periods of high prices, for this time there was no exceptional shortage of goods; there was, as some of them wrote, dearth (or dearness) without scarcity. A year or two before our date, however, a solution of the mystery found its way to England in the writings of the famous French jurist Jean Bodin, who had been considering the same phenomenon in France, where it was even more pronounced. Bodin was not the first to invent this solution, but he stated it so well that it was at once accepted in England and

C

was scarcely questioned until the twentieth century.[1] He saw that prices, which express the relative values of goods and money, would undergo the same sort of change if goods became scarcer or if money became more plentiful. And money had become more plentiful. The supply of the precious metals, in particular of silver, which was the principal monetary metal, had been increasing for some time. In the fifteenth century many new silver mines had been worked in Central Europe, and gold had begun to come in from West Africa. Soon both gold and silver had trickled in from America. In 1545 the Spaniards discovered the great silver-mines at Potosí in Upper Peru (now in Bolivia). The trickle became a river. In 1571 the application of a new method of extracting silver from the ore turned it into a torrent. The world's production of silver was perhaps six times as great in 1572 as it was in 1496.

It is indeed true that the economy of various European countries, and of England among them, had for some time past needed greater supplies of money. The rise of money economy meant that more coin was needed for paying rents and taxes and official salaries, for hiring mercenary soldiers, for handling goods in the markets. If the influx of silver had merely kept pace with this rising demand there would have been no change in the general level of prices; but it outpaced demand, and not only that, it came into Europe not like a shower equally distributed over the surface, but like a flood, rising highest in Spain and checked by the dykes of geographical distance and national economic barriers before it spilled over into other countries.

[1] Except that the matter was complicated by the debasements of the coinage, for which see below, pp. 81-3.

Prices rose so high in Spain that foreigners could bring home fantastic profits by selling there, until the price-level in their own countries rose to equal that of Spain. The process was retarded in some places by accidental circumstances, such as wars against Spain; and, of course, the more of the new silver a country could absorb by extending the sphere of money economy, the less its price-level rose. But, with many delays and complications, it did come about that England, France, the Low Countries, Italy, Poland and Germany sold their goods to Spain, and then to one another, for greatly increased quantities of the precious metals, and this led to a general rise in prices, though this rise was smaller and more gradual in the other countries than in Spain.

In modern language this influx of money was a long-continued process of inflation. It therefore had profound effects in economic life. It was favourable to all those who had to make payments over a period of time in fixed sums of money, and unfavourable to those who had to accept these payments. The tenant could get more for his corn in the market, and so it cost him less in labour to earn his rent; but the landlord could buy less with his rents when they came in. The merchant could get more for his cargo, and so it cost him less to find the interest for the sleeping partners who financed his voyage, but their money was worth less to them when they got it. Thus debtors were favoured at the expense of creditors; traders came off better than landowners; agricultural producers were strongly attracted by the profits of the market. When they spent their profits, to be sure they had to pay higher prices for everything they bought; but as prices still went on rising they could make good their higher expenses by still more profits. Again, although the long-term creditor suffered, there was money to be made by lending to the producer or trader who wanted finance: profits provided money for investment and so it was possible to expand business by borrowing. Thus there was an increase of wealth and production all round, a reinforcement of all the expansive tendencies, especially that of money economy. Yet the change was so sudden and so uncontrolled that to many, from great noblemen down to poor labourers, it brought bewildering hardship and even disaster.

Before we look more closely at the social consequences of this change or at the measures by which statesmen tried to influence them, we must consider a second great change. This originated outside the economic system: it was the great religious change which we call the Protestant Reformation. From the beginning of the ecclesiastical revolution until our own time many writers have traced connexions between it and economic changes. It was natural that the adherents of the old religion should blame the innovators for all the evils of the new age, but some of their arguments, and many of those used on the same side at the present day, require no more formal answer than the parody of an Elizabethan ballad-maker:

When that we had the old law a merry[1] world was then
And everything was plenty amongst all sorts of men.
I tell thee what, good fellow, before the monks went hence
A bushel of the best wheat was sold for fourteen pence.

But there are two directions in which religious changes did influence English economy. The first is in the

[1] This word means 'pleasant': the phrase 'Merry England' does not imply any abnormal jollity among our ancestors.

sphere of the mind. The Church of England was divided from that of Rome. The opinions and practices of Anglicans were by no means uniform; indeed, the differences between the Puritans and the other more conservative elements were already acute. The new streams of thought which were flowing in from different sides brought with them many unfamiliar views of human life and destiny. Types of character and conduct were now admired and imitated which had not previously been held up to admiration, and they found expression in the economic sphere as well as in those of religious observances and personal relations. Puritanism tried to impose a severe discipline on the laity, and it also exalted the degree of sanctity which could be attained by a layman, not specially dedicated like the 'religious' of the Roman Church to a life withdrawn from the world. Its discipline in economic matters was still directed against avarice, and towards upholding, by ecclesiastical penalties as well as by the secular action of Christian rulers, the old conceptions of wealth as a trust and of justice and charity as social duties. Puritanism was, however, associated in a number of ways with the business world and with the middle strata of rural society: its roots were in the Continental cities, and it converted most easily the men who were least satisfied with things as they had been, or most accustomed to make their fortunes by striking out for themselves. Thus it probably gave a new emphasis to the idea, old enough in itself, that work was a religious duty. The medieval monks had taught that to labour was to pray; and there is a text in Ecclesiasticus about men whose prayer is 'in the handiwork of their craft'; but perhaps this conception was now spreading to embrace the competitive efforts of the organizers and merchants. On the other hand, there was perhaps less sympathy and less indulgence for the poor. The *Book of Homilies* exhorts the faithful to works of charity, but it deals severely with the sin of idleness.

How far this change of attitude had gone, and what effect it had on actual economic relations no one can say: however many sayings and opinions are collected, the conclusion from them cannot be anything but an impressionistic guess. It may have smoothed the way for a change in the law regarding usury. When this matter was put before the great Reformer Calvin he reluctantly gave his views. How little he wished to press them is shown by this, that they occupy only two pages in more than twenty volumes of the best edition of his collected works. Dismissing, as well he might, the old arguments of principle against usury, he declared that usury was permissible except where it was oppressive or contrary to the common utility; but, although he allowed it in principle and restricted it by making exceptions, he was no more lax and no less charitable than the writers who forbade it in principle and permitted it by exceptions. He demonstrated that usury as such was no more covetous than many practices, such as mortgages, which no one condemned. In England the official view was still against usury in principle: in this year 1572 a distinguished man of affairs who was both an ecclesiastic and a jurist, Thomas Wilson, published a prolix *Discourse upon Usury* in which he mentions Calvin, but neither recites his argument nor attempts to answer it.

The theory of the lawyers and the divines had no longer any effect on business practice. In 1545 an Act of Parliament, of which the preamble stated that

he existing laws against usury were of no effect,
permitted the taking of interest so long as it did not
exceed 10 per cent. In 1552 another Act, passed by
the Protestant Parliament under Protector Northumberland, repealed it and restored the old prohibition.
In 1571 usury was made legal again, and 10 per cent
was again fixed as the maximum rate of interest. In the
Parliamentary debate on this Act, Dr. Wilson and a
number of speakers, Protestants though they were,
gave the old arguments for the old doctrine. The legal
limitation of the rate of interest was destined to last
on paper for centuries, and we know that in its later
days it was completely ineffective: the lawyers easily
found ways of evading it. We have no reason to think
that it was more effective in its earlier days than in its
later. We know that Henry VII and Henry VIII and
their subjects paid interest on loans before 1545, and
that money-lending of many kinds went on uninter-
ruptedly from 1552 to 1571. The purpose of the two
Acts of 1545 and 1571 was to depress the rate of
interest so as to enable the Government to borrow at
10 per cent, which was lower than the rate prevailing
in the market. They resulted not from a change in
moral outlook, but from a desire for cheap money;
and the same desire on the part of the papacy and of
Catholic governments led in the same century to
comparable changes in the law in some Continental
countries. In Catholic Italy and South Germany and
the Netherlands capitalism in all its aspects developed
far earlier than in England. We know that the deliberately expressed disapproval of Catholic theologians
failed to dissuade business men from making contracts
which were both technically and really usurious. So
far as the development of credit transactions was

impeded by social causes, we must ascribe a much smaller influence to opinion against usury than to social insecurity, the hazards of transport and communications and the restricted scale of organization. And we must not draw a contrast in this respect between the countries which now broke away from Rome and those which did not.

The Reformation had definite and immediate economic effects, not in the sphere of belief and conduct, but where it interfered with property. In England it brought about the greatest transferences of land-ownership since the Norman Conquest. First, Henry VIII confiscated the whole of the property of the monasteries, to the value of more than £1,000,000. Then Edward VI took lands worth more than a tenth of this tremendous sum, those of the 'chantries', endowments for prayers and masses in parish churches and chapels and in charitable foundations. At the end of his reign an attack was begun on some of the episcopal lands. It had not gone very far when it was suspended by the accession of the Catholic Mary; but Queen Elizabeth resumed it. By an Act of Parliament she took some of the bishops' 'temporalities', or landed estates, in exchange for less valuable 'spiritualities', tithes transferred from the monasteries. Their value does not seem ever to have been calculated. These enormous changes of ownership had effects which ran through the whole economic structure of the country. It was not that large numbers of peasants and gentlemen ceased to have indulgent clerical landlords: the monasteries on the whole managed their estates more acquisitively than lay landowners. The great economic fact was that a large proportion of the nation's wealth, previously locked up in the ownership of bodies which went on from century to century and never died, was suddenly flung on the market. The Crown took the land because it needed money, and it needed money so badly that it could not simply add the Church lands to the Crown lands and so increase its permanent revenues by the new rents. That would have necessitated an administrative revolution, and, besides its immediate need for money, the Crown had a political reason for not holding what it took. In order to commit them to supporting his religious changes, Henry VIII handed over most of the monastic lands to noblemen or gentlemen. A few of them got free grants, but most of them had to pay for what they bought. These great sales did not end with Henry VIII and Edward VI, for Queen Elizabeth's debts and expenses were so great that in the first five or six years of her reign she had to sell some of her own lands, to the value of more than a quarter of a million. Thus land was now bought and sold on a far greater scale than before, and the new state of things perpetuated itself, for the buyers were subject to time and chance, and often enough they or their heirs had to sell in their turn. This meant a multiplication of the amount of property bought and sold, a great extension in the sphere of money economy.

We know little about the history of these transactions. It looks as if the Crown disposed of its new assets so hurriedly that it may not have got as good prices as could have been realized by gradual sales; but there is some reason to think that in fact these lands brought in at least twenty years' purchase—that is, twenty times their annual rental value—which was considered then and for long afterwards a normal price. Whether that is so or not, enormous sums of purchase money were raised by the business men, the merchants and financiers. They formed syndicates to buy the property in large parcels, afterwards selling as opportunity offered either in the same units or piecemeal. Thus the business world, or, roughly speaking, the City of London, was able to find hundreds of thousands of pounds to invest in trading in land. The ultimate purchasers seem to have been partly men who had made money in commerce and industry or in the service of the Crown, partly rural landlords or members of their families, including many who had been associated with the monasteries as stewards or agents for their property. In wealth they ranged from large landowners like the Russells, Saviles, Cavendishes, Portmans, Pagets, and Thynnes to small squires. We know little about how they financed their purchases. It would not be surprising if many of them left part of the price on mortgage to be paid off gradually out of income. If they did so, or even if they scraped the purchase money together by selling whatever they could convert into cash, they had a strong motive for screwing as much rent as they could out of their tenants. We know of some new owners of monastic property who were harsh and exacting landlords; but we have no means of knowing whether, as has sometimes been suggested, those who came from trade were more oppressive than the older feudal landlords. After all, in that age landowning and land management were as much matters of business as trade or industry. Walter of Henley's book was printed by Wynkyn de Worde; but it was soon superseded by the *Husbandry* and *Surveyenge* of a judge named Fitzherbert, published in 1523 and 1539, which gave practical precepts to tenants on how to support their families and to landlords on how to protect themselves in their rights. Nor was it only the

new landlords who had a strong motive for raising
rents. As we have seen, the price revolution lowered
the value of all fixed money dues, and the most obvious
way for a landowner to escape its effects was to convert
his leases into annual tenancies at rack-rents.

Doubtless the price revolution and the expansion
of the real estate market interacted in many ways.
Between them they account for many distinctive
features of English rural economy. The freeholders'
small rents vanished: they could easily be bought off
for good. By 1572 villeinage had practically dis-
appeared. In its last days it had been criticized on
moral grounds. Fitzherbert, for instance, wrote: 'as
me seemeth there should be no man bounde but to
God, and to his kynge, and prince over him'. But it
was cash, not charity, that made it possible to extinguish villein services. Again, in France many
landowners protected themselves against the fall in
the value of money by taking their rents in kind: under
the system of *métayage*, the tenant kept half his produce
and paid half to the landlord. In England that system
was known, but it never became common, because
both landlord and tenant were accustomed to handling
money. A tenant-farmer in Henry VIII's time wrote:

> Rent-corn whoso payeth (as worldlings would have
> So much for an acre) must work like a slave;
> Rent-corn to be paid for a reas'nable rent
> At reas'nable prices, is not to lament.

That is to say, he did not mind paying in corn, but the
rent and the value of the corn were both to be fixed
by a money standard.

Among the social effects of the dissolution of the
monasteries, the greatest was the consolidation of the

body of the gentry. The small and moderately wealthy squires were now more numerous; many of them were convinced supporters of the ecclesiastical revolution to which they owed their estates, and as a body they played a great part in the energetic administration of Tudor England, as well as in the wars by land and sea. Such men were the Grenvilles and Raleighs of the West Country. The Tudors believed in 'degree'. They did not discourage the ambition to rise from one level to another; indeed, they had done it themselves, for the Queen was descended on her father's side from a Welsh knight, Owen Tudor, and on her mother's from Geoffrey Boleyn, who was Lord Mayor of London in 1457. The catechism made every child promise, not, as many people think, to do his duty in that station in life to which it had pleased God to call him or her, but 'in that state of life unto which it shall please God to call me'. The Elizabethan statesman, Sir Thomas Smith, wrote, probably in 1565, a survey of the system of ranks. No man was created a baron unless he might spend at least 1,000 marks, or two thirds of £1,000, yearly. Of the lesser nobility or gentlemen, anyone who could spend £40 a year from his free lands might still be compelled to become a knight or to pay a fine.[1] Below this it was not the king who conferred rank; gentlemen were noble by 'blood and race', but 'they be made good cheap in England', and all were taken for gentlemen who had studied at the universities, who practised liberal professions, or in general who lived without manual labour and kept up something of a position. The Tudor kings and queens encouraged

[1] This means a payment which settles a transaction or dispute: in this context and some others (for instance, on pp. 73, 94 of this book), it has not the sense familiar to us of a payment imposed as a punishment.

the College of Heralds, which had the duty of seeing that no one used a coat of arms, the distinguishing mark of gentility, without a right to it. In 1530 the heralds allowed this right to any man with good honest reputation together with lands and possessions of free tenure to the yearly value of £10 or in movable goods £300.

A new series of Acts of Apparel began in the first year of Henry VIII and went on until the time we speak of. They were no better observed than those of the Middle Ages, though the machinery for enforcing them was improved; for instance, one of Elizabeth's reign mentions the subsidy-books as the sources of information about people's incomes. They had various purposes,[1] including that of protecting industry. A new Act in 1571 ordered that all persons above the age of six, except lords, knights, gentlemen of 20 marks in land and their heirs, and those who had borne 'offices of worship' in towns and villages, etc., and their families, were to wear a woollen cap of English manufacture on Sundays and holy days. This was the only Act which said what people must wear; the others all said what people of different ranks must not wear; their chief purpose was to regulate these distinctions, and the chief dividing lines were still the different degrees of peerage, the office of mayor, the possession of £200 or £100 and 40s. a year. The 40s. freeholder was still for Sir Thomas Smith, who called him a 'yeoman', the lowest member of the governing classes, above 'the fourth sort of men which do not rule'. He confessed himself to be no gentleman, and yet had more

---

[1] Their effect on consumption was negligible, as was that of the curious Acts of 1548, 1563, and 1603 which, in order to encourage the fisheries, made Lenten and other fish-days compulsory notwithstanding the Reformation.

estimation than labourers and artificers and commonly lived 'wealthily'. For the most part, besides having their own land, yeomen were 'farmers unto gentlemen', and they daily bought the lands of unthrifty gentlemen, so that their sons, to whom they left the lands, went to the universities or into the law and became gentlemen.

In this rural society, where some men were making money while others were losing it, one kind of change was visible to the naked eye, the enclosure of fields by making new hedges. It was going on for a variety of reasons on different kinds of land in many parts of the country. Rich men were making parks for their deer; orchards were being enclosed in the cider counties of the Severn Basin; in East Anglia enterprising farmers made closes for industrial crops like madder and flax: in the neighbourhood of a town it might pay to enclose waste land or even old arable land for dairy farming. There is no doubt that a capable farmer, whatever type of farming he followed, could get a better yield from land held 'in severalty' than from the complicated combination of common rights and strips in the untidy common fields. The enclosure of both waste and common fields had been going on, as we have seen, here and there for centuries. It always involved the rearrangement or abandonment of the local customary common rights, rotations of crops and so forth; it always meant more uncontrolled management of his land by the landlord or the tenant or both; it often brought hardships for the poor.

From the time of Henry VII the government came to regard one special type of enclosure as a major element in the social problem. This was the enclosure of open-field townships for the purpose of sheep-farming. If a landowner, by fair means or foul, got control of the whole land of the village and turned it into a sheep-run, he might make a great profit out of wool, the most important of all English industrial raw materials; but the land would give employment to far fewer hands. Consequently, the government heard with alarm of villages falling into ruin; of dwindling musters for the militia; of parishes where the tithe no longer supported the priest. First an Act against depopulation was passed for the Isle of Wight, vitally important for defence against France; then in 1489 came the first of a series of Acts applying to the whole realm, forbidding landowners under penalties to convert arable land into pasture or to allow farmhouses or cottages to fall into decay. The Crown not only pushed this legislation through Parliament; Wolsey and Protector Somerset sent out strong Commissions to inquire into the enforcement of the law and the actual progress of enclosures. They found that it was easy to evade the statutes. At various times and in different parts of the country there was anger among the common people. They did not protest only against those changes which gave concern to the king's ministers; parks were a grievance for them, but they were encouraged by authority. But depopulation was as hard on the poor as it was dangerous to the realm, so that the Crown, the villagers and the literary men, though they did not altogether agree, were more or less united against the growth of sheep-farming.

In most of the popular risings of the Tudor period there were some agrarian complaints in the lists of grievances, and the East Anglian rebellion of Ket, which wrecked the reforming attempts of Protector

Somerset, had a programme, apparently moderate, though hard to understand, of agrarian conservatism. Like all the other popular revolts of the Tudor period, it failed, and ended in greater freedom for the oppressors. Queen Elizabeth, in the fifth year of her reign, re-enacted the laws of Henry VII and Henry VIII against enclosure; but there is no reason to suppose that her Act was enforced any better than the others.

The best modern authorities are disposed to think that the legislation and the administrative efforts consequent on it acted as a brake, retarding though not preventing the enclosures, and probably also mitigating the harshness of their effects on the small man. Until much detailed research has been done on separate regions, it will be impossible to estimate the general progress of enclosure in Tudor times; but apparently it was only in the English Midlands that it went on at a revolutionary pace. In the counties of Leicester, Northampton, and Rutland and the south-eastern portion of Warwickshire, and to a slightly lower degree in Bedfordshire, Berkshire, Buckinghamshire, and Oxfordshire, there was a great increase in the proportion of pasture to arable. Even in Cambridgeshire and Huntingdonshire, which remained predominantly counties of mixed farming, the increase was considerable. It was large in Middlesex, no doubt because of the needs of London. Except in Middlesex it went hand in hand with depopulation. We do not know what became of the displaced workers. Some, no doubt, followed the wool into the industrial towns of the Cotswolds and East Anglia. Others joined the army of unemployed and vagrants. We do not know whether enclosure was as important in its general social effects as some other agrarian changes of the ime. The price revolution seems to have caused a widespread substitution of variable for fixed fines on admission to copyholds; many copyholds were conerted into leases for lives[1] or for fixed terms of years. These changes enabled the landlord to take the large unearned increment in the money value of produce which otherwise would have stayed in the tenant's pocket. They made it easier to evict tenants and so to build up large farms and large estates; but we do not now whether in some or many parts of the country the usual size of farms and estates other than sheepruns was increasing. We may presume that the relations of landlord and tenant were coming to be based more on the strict letter of the law; and this must have been a change to the disadvantage of the small man, though there were still opportunities for the squatter and the grasping peasant.

Everything that we do know about the agrarian history of the period points to an extension of money economy—that is, of farming for the market, of division of labour and specialization in the purposes of farms. Broadly speaking, this means that aggregate production increased, as it must have done, since population was increasing. To this extent the enclosures represented a rationalization of farming, or an increase in efficiency. The country was, however, still thinly populated; communications were primitive, and there was no need and no attempt to wring the utmost possible product out of the soil. There was still so much space available that inhabited places could be emptied without creating congestion on the land.

[1] Three persons were generally named in such a lease, which held good as long as any of them survived. This sporting system only died out within living memory.

England still had conditions like those of an economic 'frontier' where new land is available for cultivation. Agriculture was less intensive than in the Low Countries or Normandy, and the growing demand of the home market was satisfied by a limited, if reluctant, movement of workers from place to place and from one occupation to another, without much change in agricultural knowledge or methods, and without any great change in organization except for the continued spread of money economy.

The forces of economic change did not operate gradually and steadily. We have already seen that there were ups and downs, that the course of business was, as it has been ever since this time, subject to fluctuations. Two special causes of these fluctuations must be mentioned. First, there were wars. When the government went to war it had to find much larger sums of money than in peace and the scale of war was increasing. Henry VIII spent not far short of £1,000,000 on the expeditions of his early years, far more than any English king had spent in so short a time, in addition to considerable subsidies to the emperor for his military purposes. Henry and his successor spent more than two millions on the war of 1542–7; the next war, in 1547–50, cost more than another million. Queen Mary's war expenditure was less in amount, but Queen Elizabeth in her long reign spent more than five millions on warlike purposes: she had already spent a million before 1572.

These sums do not represent the full cost of the wars to the nation, for not all the expenses were paid by the Crown. The clothing, pay and equipment of troops so long as they were in England were found by local

uthorities. Some of the operations at sea were carried
n by privateers, ships fitted out by private owners who
eld commissions from the Crown and recouped
hemselves by taking a stated share, or more than
heir stated share, of their prizes. But the sums
vhich had to be provided by taxation or loans to
he Crown so far exceeded the ordinary revenue
hat it was always hard to raise them, and public
inance made such demands on the capacity of the
ountry that, as we shall see later, private finance, and
ousiness generally, fluctuated accordingly. It was not
only that the State had to find large sums of money.
The spending of this money also had its results. We
ave seen how the industries connected with firearms
vere stimulated. This stimulus was, of course, fitful;
vith peace it fell off; and so did the demand for cloth-
ng and victuals for soldiers and sailors. Thus there
vere war booms in the supplying industries; but at
the same time war, by interrupting sea transport and
foreign trade and by diverting men from production
to the armies, brought depression in other quarters.

The movement from depression to boom and back
again through crisis to depression was brought about
in these two opposite ways by war, but it was familiar
in other directions as well. The upward movement in
itself needs no special explanation. The profits gained
in the markets fertilized further production. This
process might be accentuated by some special access
of demand like that for munitions, or by some wider
favouring condition like that of the price-revolution.
But it always depended on the continuing expansion
of the market, and therefore any check or stoppage in
that might turn the boom into a glut, when prices fell
and it was impossible to sell except at a loss, and so

again impossible to buy as much as before. Thus, as everyone in business sold in order to buy, and bought in order to sell, each man who limited his operations brought others down with him, and the depression spread in a widening circle, until no one could buy or sell more than bare necessities, and, then, when buying and selling had touched bottom, the cyclical movement began again.

The alternation between scarcity and glut was as old as trading itself, and it happened in a dozen ways. A bad harvest had the greatest effect of all: even if corn sold dear, the farmers as a whole made so little profit that the clothiers and pewterers and potters could sell nothing. Perhaps, the changes from war to peace and back again already had effects which ran through the whole community in the same way. On the other hand the cycle might run its course in a limited sphere: it might effect one locality or one group of occupations without extending to others. In a peasant society, with poor transport and undeveloped natural resources, it did so more often than in a modern society. Thus if a nobleman's rents came in badly and he had to stop work on his new country house, the stonemason could go off to his farm, or with luck could find a piece of waste land to break in. But it appears that in the Tudor age these possibilities were becoming rarer. More was said about vagrancy and sturdy beggars, so much more that it seems that it was becoming generally harder for men thrown out of employment to find other kinds of work. We do not know with any certainty why this was so. Since the late eighteenth-century historians have usually held that 'the decrease of villeinage seems necessarily to have been the era of the origins of the Poor'. At any rate, the poor law

ecame much more positive and comprehensive: it
rovided increasingly effective public assistance where
here had been only private and religious charity.
rom 1531 the justices of the peace took a hand in it
nd conditions were laid down under which 'aged,
oor and impotent persons' might solicit alms. From
536 each parish was responsible for collecting alms
nd relieving its own poor; from 1563 contributions
ere made compulsory. The City of London had
ready begun experiments in providing work for the
ole-bodied poor, and in a codifying Act of 1572 there
as the feeble beginning of a general permission to
cal authorities to do this.

There were so many changes in the law that it
vidently had not yet solved the problem, and we
annot analyse the problem as we can similar problems
a later times which we can state in terms of figures.
arliament only met at irregular intervals, so it is
nisleading to think that changes in the law adequately
nirror the fluctuations of social and economic
onditions. Perhaps there was more unemployment.
More was written about it in books and pamphlets;
nuch attention was paid to it in parliament and
ouncil; but printing was a growing trade, and the
tate was raising its standard of law and order. The
nclosures may have added to the numbers of un-
mployed; at times there were discharged soldiers and
ailors; the manufacturing for export may have in-
reased the numbers of those who depended on the
ncertainties of foreign markets. Again, there may
ave been less new land to absorb the unemployed.
s we have no statistics for any of these matters we
nust leave them in doubt.

We have to leave it in doubt exactly how closely knit

society had become; but the nucleus which was kn
together by money economy was spreading so as t
make the cyclical movements run into one another an
become waves of prosperity or depression affecting
larger and larger proportion of the population. Whe
business can call credit to its aid, its power of expansio
is increased and the business man looks on his credit
not as a usurer and an enemy but as a fellow capitalis
In England in the sixteenth century the markets f
so many kinds of goods expanded that the mone
market, which fed them all with capital, expanded to
More people made it their business to deal in mone
so that borrowing was less a mere touting roun
among those who might have money to spare. Th
money market was in some ways very well organize
In London it was in the hands of substantial men wh
were experts in specialized branches. The goldsmith
whose company assayed and stamped all gold an
silver plate, had gone into banking with the profits
their trade behind them. The scriveners in th
fourteenth century had been concerned with drawir
up certain kinds of documents; from that some of the
had moved on to providing the money to which th
documents referred. A few experts dealt in foreig
exchange, though the Crown from time to time ha
tried to reduce them to the position of mere inte
mediaries by appointing an exchanger, with a monopo
in this field, who was to control the exchanges in th
interests, first and foremost, of the Crown as borrowe
The money-market was an international market, an
that meant that Continental wealth, far greater tha
that of England, could be drawn upon to finan
government and business in England. It meant al
that the provision of finance for English purposes wa

o some extent on a broader basis than that of merely national prosperity: when there was a shortage of money in England, there might yet be enough to pay the interest on loans from abroad. This fortunate state of things was due above all to the rise of Antwerp. With that centre of European commerce the English traders had their regular commerce in bills of exchange, and the English money-market was almost an overseas branch of the Antwerp market.

All this was favourable to expansion, but it had corresponding dangers. The more business depends on the money-market, the more the fluctuations of the money-market make themselves felt throughout all business. At this time the money-market was liable to large fluctuations. They might come about like fluctuations in any other market, by an excess or a deficiency of supply, by a rise or a fall of demand. The price revolution was on the whole, from the monetary point of view, a healthy movement; but during the same period the money-markets had some sharp attacks of disease. The greatest operators in the money-markets, both national and international, were governments, and their operations were sudden and disturbing. They seldom lent and when they borrowed they often defaulted. At home they could force the lenders to provide money, often on bad security; in the international market, they could not all do this. Fortunately for their country, the kings and queens of England could not borrow beyond the credit of the City; but others, especially the kings of Spain, who were sovereign in Antwerp, borrowed more there than they could ever pay, and a series of crises in the second half of the century shook the whole international system of credit.

We may now sketch the action of English governments in economic matters from 1496 to 1572. Public
finance need not detain us long: we have already
noticed the chief innovations in raising revenue, and
the two chief reasons why more revenue had to be
raised, the price revolution and the wars. We must
now add some details. Henry VII in the last years of
his life improved the revenue. He issued the first
Book of Rates for the customs; he lent fairly large sums
to Italian merchants without interest, but on condition
of their importing goods to yield specified sums in
duties. He worked up the land revenue and let out
his ships for hire. It is impossible to say how far his
notorious agents Empson and Dudley exceeded the
law, but, by fair means or foul, Henry died with a
'treasure' which may have been in the region of a
million.

Henry VIII had Empson and Dudley beheaded,
nevertheless, he spent more than his father even in
times of peace. In Wolsey's time war and foreign
affairs were very expensive. The expenditure of the
royal household was drastically reduced, and Wolsey
got all he could from lay and clerical taxes, and also
from loans, voluntary and forced. He could not get
enough, and he hoped to make ends meet by the payments he extracted from France; but the French king
found a suitable opportunity to default, and when
Wolsey fell the financial position, though not critical
was bad. Thomas Cromwell, a successful business
man, came to the rescue and told Henry how to become
the richest prince in Christendom. His prescription
the dissolution of the monasteries, was adopted, and
for the moment it perhaps doubled the net normal
revenue of the Crown. A new 'treasure' was gathered

but fresh difficulties supervened. Prices began to rise, and in 1542, as we have seen, a costly war began. To cope with this, direct taxation was much more successful than in the earlier periods of the reign: higher rates, stricter collection and rising resources may all have contributed to this. But Henry had to borrow heavily in Antwerp: at his death £75,000 was due there, though none of it was overdue. The loans were raised in close connexion with dealings in lead and tin outwards; in alum, jewels, fustians, and copper inwards. Henry also resorted to the risky expedient of debasing the coinage. From May 1544 to the end of his reign the mint made a profit of £363,000. That is to say the coin circulating in the country (of which Thomas Cromwell had calculated the value in 1523 at a million) was over-valued by this amount. The amount was confiscated from the buying and selling community, and the loss was spread over that community in proportion to the cash held by each individual or firm at the moment.

During the first part of the reign of Edward VI the same methods were continued. At the end of the war of 1550 about a quarter of a million was owing at Antwerp, still at 14 per cent, and the mint had brought in another half million. Under Protector Northumberland the smash came. The Government was bankrupt and could pay the interest on its foreign loans only by leaving bills unpaid at home. The City of London had to guarantee fresh loans in Antwerp. Crown lands had to be sold. In the reign of Mary there were considerable financial reforms, economies all round, a simplification of machinery, a better loan policy, though the City would only lend at 12 per cent and on the security of land. A survey of the Crown

lands was ordered, and it was discussed whether they
should be farmed out as a whole for a fixed rent; but
instead of this it was decided to increase the rents and
to tighten up the terms of leases and dues. In the
customs a decline of revenue was corrected by a new
Book of Rates. The last Book, that of 1545, was out
of date because it was based on the prices of 1507, and
because it had been left behind by the change in trade,
the decline of wool exports and the rise in the exports
of cloth and beer and the re-exporting of wine. All the
Marian reforms were carried further under Elizabeth,
with the result that the land again took first place in the
permanent revenue. A new kind of tax on land and
other property, called a subsidy, was introduced alongside of the old tenths and fifteenths, but in practice it was
not different from an increase in the amount of these.

At Elizabeth's accession the debt was £227,000, of
which £107,000 was owed abroad. Throughout the
reign ordinary expenditure was kept low, though there
were some extravagances connected with the court. If
there had been no wars or rebellions the revenues
would have been more than sufficient. As it was, the
reign began with rearmament, the purchases of
munitions in the Netherlands being used as leverage
for fresh loans there. The expeditions to Scotland
and Havre in 1561 were paid for and the debt reduced
partly by sales of Crown lands. After that a beginning
was made in accumulating a reserve. The rebellion
of the Northern earls in 1579 checked the process, but
after that great efforts were made to reduce debt. We
do not know exactly how much had been achieved
by 1572; but two years later the debt had been as good
as liquidated and there was a reserve of nearly £300,000
in hand. Queen Elizabeth's ministers had not used

ovel devices of any importance from the financial
oint of view. Their patents of monopoly brought in
nly small sums[1]. Their success was due to good
management on the old lines. Their greatest single
peration was the restoration of the coinage.

Although, as we have seen, the State was still unable
o alter the main changes of economic life, ministers
were becoming more ambitious to control them. There
was a phrase 'the manor of England', as though the
Crown's revenues were like the yield of one vast
state, and as though the way to increase them was to
make the estate more prosperous. Neither of these
ideas bore much relation to the confused reality.
Early in the reign of Elizabeth the famous Statute of
Artificers (sometimes called the Statute of Apprentices)
was passed, and this, together with the tariff, laws to
encourage ship-building, the Acts against enclosures
and the poor law constituted an economic code. On
paper it was the most thoroughgoing attempt to control
the economic life of a country that any European
government had made, and it differed from the
economic legislation of Continental countries in paying
far more attention than they did to agriculture. It
embodied few if any new principles, but it aimed at
co-ordinating the existing law and administrative
machinery. Its professed aims were to banish idleness,
to advance husbandry and to yield to the hired person,
both in times of scarcity and in times of plenty, a
convenient proportion of wages. That is to say, it
had in view the three problems of unemployment, the
scarcity of agricultural labour, and the rise in the cost
of living, three aspects of the maladjustment caused by

[1] See below, p. 120.

industrialization and the rise in prices. The existing machinery had as its foundation a judiciary, the municipal courts of the towns and the justices of the peace in the country. These not only enforced in the first instance the laws relating to guilds, apprenticeship, employment, and vagrancy, but also carried out the administrative duty of fixing maximum wages. Above these local authorities stood the king's judges and the Privy Council.

The new legislation accepted and even furthered money economy: it carried forward the limiting of truck, or paying wages in kind. But the general tendency of these enactments was conservative: they aimed at providing an adequate supply of labour first for agriculture, then for the simpler crafts, and at restricting entry into the occupations of higher social standing and into those which were thought to be carried on in unsuitable places. A universal duty to work was assumed. Unmarried women between the ages of twelve and forty had to work if required to do so by two justices or by municipal authority; all fit artificers and other persons had to do harvest work if required to do so by two justices; all men from twelve to sixty not otherwise employed had to serve in husbandry if required to do so merely by employers; in certain crafts unmarried trained men and married men under thirty were similarly at the bidding of employers. Permits were required for transference from one employer to another. On the other hand, in the towns continuity of employment was to be ensured by contracts for a year's employment, and, with certain exceptions, apprenticeship was made compulsory, so that the recruiting of labour was regulated, in the urban occupations and even in agriculture.

Entry into the higher occupations was restricted according to social rank. Gentlemen born and persons having lands worth £10 a year or chattels worth £40 might apprentice their sons to merchants, etc.; those with lands of £3 might apprentice their sons in market towns; those with lands of 40s. or goods worth £10 might apprentice their sons to cloth-weavers. The number of apprentices, and their rank by birth, were similarly defined, and in such a way as to protect the corporate towns against the competition of mere market-towns and of rural industry. The decay of corporate towns had been alleged as a motive in one of the economic statutes of Philip and Mary; and though, no doubt, there may have been local economic reasons for it in special instances, if there was a general cause, it was the movement of industry to rural areas where it was free from the restrictions of guilds and corporations. Such migrations had taken place in the Low Countries, and the English guilds had resisted this tendency from time to time for centuries past.

It is not clear how the Tudor legislation was dovetailed with the existing guild-system. The national statutes contained no general provisions compelling all craftsmen to belong to their appropriate guilds, though this was provided for in some particular trades. But the corporations held their rights by charter, and Parliament took the existence of these charters for granted. Thus the Statute of Artificers did not fix the number of apprentices in proportion to the number of journeymen allowed to a single employer, except for the textile trades and shoe-making; but in other trades the local guild regulations imposed such restrictions. Since the time of Henry VII (1504) the king's courts of law had exercised control over guild regulations, as indeed the justices of the peace have done before them, and this means that the guilds and corporations acted under the authority of the State. We know that within twenty years of their enactment the corporations administered the apprenticeship clauses of the Statute of Artificers, and it is reasonable to suppose that they did so from the beginning.

The Elizabethan code thus aimed at stabilizing the existing class-structure, the location of industry and the flow of labour supply by granting privileges and by putting hindrances in the way of mobility and freedom of contract; but it was not the product of a simple doctrinaire economic policy; it reconciled or effected a compromise between conflicting interests. The provisions in favour of corporate towns were there no doubt because the corporate towns were represented in Parliament. Some amendments were made in Parliament which limited the effect of the law. A large part of the nation's economic life was never touched at all by the restrictive code. Noblemen, gentlemen and others, as employers in their households, were left quite free; so too were seamen, fishermen, the dealers and carriers who supplied London with corn and other food, and employers in mining, the metal trades and glass-making. In a number of very important trades there was no limitation on the social origin of apprentices: these were the building trades and those of smiths, wheelwrights, ploughwrights, some classes of weavers, turners, coopers, millers, potters, fullers, smelters, and charcoal-burners. The Statute of Artificers also excepted certain localities from the restrictions on the textile trades. In Wales and the north-west, which were comparatively poor and undeveloped, weavers might take as apprentices anyone hey could find. The custom of London, permitting movement between trades, was explicitly recognized.

Even from the first the Elizabethan code did not amount to a general revival of the restrictive tendency or a general checking of the tendency to expansion; and the expansive tendency soon made breaches in the dyke erected against it. The judges who decided cases arising under these laws acted on the principle that trade was to be restrained only by explicit enactments: where nothing was said against it, the presumption was that any particular economic activity was lawful. Thus the restrictions of the Statute of Artificers applied only to the trades which were practised in the country at the time of its enactment, and the new industries which were introduced in quick succession after it were able to grow up without any limitations of apprenticeship, labour contracts, or locality.

When a government was trying to keep up the foreign value of the pound sterling in order to borrow cheaply abroad, it could not afford to encourage exports; when it was trying to increase its revenue from the Customs, it was tempted to tax all imports and all exports without regard to any plan for encouraging some and discouraging others; when it called for free gifts or forced loans, or even for the greatest possible parliamentary taxation, it could pay no regard to the need for capital in agriculture or industry or trade. A special cause of confusion and self-contradiction in policy was that, as we have seen, the easiest method of protectionism was to give special privileges to trading companies. The companies had far greater knowledge of foreign trade than the governments; they had more representatives and more personal connexions abroad.

It was easier for governments to deal with them than with unorganized bodies of traders, and they could offer the governments, not only technical advice, but ready money, whether as loans or gifts or as duties on the goods they passed through the ports. Governments, since they nearly always want to bring about some immediate result, have strong reasons for dealing with those who have power, and for helping them to increase their power. Business combinations want to increase their power, and often they want to do it by expanding their businesses competitively—by capturing trade from foreigners, for instance. Thus the companies took part in the Tudor policy of economic nationalism. But at times they had also a conflicting interest. Sometimes the easiest way to increase their power was by the method of monopoly: if they could absorb or extinguish their English competitors, and fix the price of the wares they sold abroad without fear of being undercut, then it became their interest not to expand, but to sell little and sell dear. To encourage the companies under these conditions was to check expansion.

Economic policy therefore wavered uncertainly between restricting and encouraging expansion. A rough distinction may be drawn between the first half of the sixteenth century and the second. In the first half the general note was comparative freedom in foreign trade, and the chief reason for it was that good relations with the thriving Low Countries satisfied English needs and stimulated English industry. After the middle of the century the English currency policy was restrictive; difficulties with the Netherlands began in 1563 and were never overcome before the decline of Antwerp, which was contemporaneous with civil war in France and many warlike interferences with navigation. Thus the English nation was driven in on itself; the privileges of the Hanse were abolished in 1552, and only partially restored in 1560; the new draperies grew up; the industrial code put a brake on enterprise; there were fresh laws for encouraging tillage. The chances of wealth from overseas seemed to depend, not on peaceable trade, but on the forays of privateering sea-dogs, and it was in this year 1572 that Drake first attacked the Spanish harbours in America.

D

CHAPTER IV

GREAT BRITAIN AND HER RIVALS, TO 1662

WHEN we moved forward from 1496 to 1572, we found signs of impending change in various directions; when we take our next step forward, from 1572 to 1662, we find that many great changes had come about. The geography of the realm was now quite different. Scotland was in personal union with England, and, although this did not make any change in the economic separateness of Scotland, in its separate currency, tariff, and so forth, it did mean that in international political affairs Great Britain was a single unit. Thus the two countries now made war and peace together; the Border between them was no longer a military frontier with special laws on each side of it and abnormal economic conditions; there was even a common citizenship and the king's subjects in either realm might hold property of any kind in the other. So far, even after sixty years, this personal union had not led to any notable change in the volume or character of the trade between the two kingdoms; but it had brought constitutional union and economic union into the sphere of political discussion. For a few years, during the Protectorate, both these kinds of union actually existed. That state of things was ended by the Restoration of Charles II in 1660; but Anglo-Scottish relations were not yet satisfactorily settled, and the statesmen who had to deal with them had their economic aspect in mind as well as the political and ecclesiastical.

The next important change was in England's

relations with Ireland. The policy of colonization, of which we saw the modest beginnings, had been pushed forward on a considerable scale, and British settlers had gone over in two waves. The first went to Ulster, and mainly in the time of James I. Since he was king of Scotland, the surplus population of that weaker state was enabled by English capital investment to move into the void created by the successes of English arms; and Ulster was filled up by both Englishmen and Scotsmen, partly under the auspices of a limited company compulsorily created by the Crown in the City of London. The second wave came into a larger area, which it settled much less densely. The original inhabitants of Ulster broke into rebellion in 1641. The final result of ten years of war in the whole of Ireland was the Cromwellian conquest, and a drastic resettlement by which only Connaught and County Clare were left wholly to the Irish, while some hundreds of British soldiers and other immigrants were settled as squires and farmers over the remainder. Ireland was now more orderly than it had been for centuries, and some able English administrators and business men were surveying its resources. Its population was probably under a million; how far under is a controversial point, but it seems likely that it was nearer three quarters of a million than half a million.

English emigration to Ireland was part of an overflow which also ran in other directions. In the first half of the seventeenth century there was a considerable movement to North America and the West Indies. By 1662 the British colonies there included Jamaica, Barbados, Bermuda, half a dozen small islands, and two groups of mainland colonies, New England in the

north, Virginia and Maryland in the south. Their
white population numbered more than 100,000,
representing an emigration of somewhere about that
number, drawn from all classes of Englishmen. As we
all know, the motives of the emigrants were mixed.
Religion played a part, though a smaller part than in
the sixteenth-century immigration into England; but
it is mainly for economic reasons that the exodus
coincided roughly in time with the reign of Charles I.
The population of England had not only overflowed:
it had grown substantially at home. Even if we had no
figures, we should have known this from various
indications, one of which was a revival of home
colonization. Both James I and Charles I, like their
ministers and some of their wealthy subjects, paid
attention to the draining of marshes. Dutch engineers
and Dutch capitalists were concerned in these projects.
They were neither so large nor so difficult as the
schemes which were carried out in Holland early in the
century; none of the English drained lands are below
high-water mark except at the spring tides; but much
work was done. In Sedgemoor, the Thames Estuary,
Hatfield Chase, and the Great Level of the Fens many
square miles of land were won. The local fishermen
and fowlers resisted these improvements, which took
away their livelihood; but in the long run they provided maintenance for a larger as well as a more
prosperous population. But there is more direct
evidence to prove that population was growing. We
have much more trustworthy figures for this period
than for earlier centuries, and we may be fairly sure
that the population was in the region of five millions
and was increasing.

We know little about the reasons for this increase.

The country was now able to support a larger number of people. As we shall see there were many other factors of economic development, besides home colonization, to account for this. We do not know, however, whether the increase of population itself improved the economic productivity of the country by making labour available where it could be best applied. Nor do we know whether there was any biological change after 1572 such as an increase in fertility. Some authorities think that the birth-rate increased about 1600 and then settled down again about 1630; but, if that is so, still we do not know how far the increase from the greater number of births was undone by a higher death-rate as it would be unless the conditions for survival became more favourable. On the whole it looks as if the death-rate for the country taken as a whole was falling. The towns were growing, and they were unhealthy, so it appears that a larger proportion of the people were living in the country, and that must mean that there was more employment there too, and far more than that which was due to the draining and clearing of new land. •

In this period we begin to get a clearer view of the growth of London. It was still out of all proportion to the other towns: Norwich, probably the second largest, had a growing population of 15,000 in 1601, while London with the liberties, including Southwark across the river, was believed to have twenty times that number. Many industries flourished there, the leather trades as Bermondsey, the minor metal trades; making locks, buckles, hooks and eyes, pins and needles, utensils; the immigrant silk-weaving in north-east London, the breweries, the glasshouses along the Thames-side, and the flour-mills along the Thames and Wandle, besides the old cloth-working and the new industry of coach-making. The city authorities asserted their rights against the liberties, and this exclusiveness led to overcrowding of every kind within the city limits. Early in Queen Elizabeth's reign most of the free sites there were built over, so that new building had to spread outwards; but the Privy Council shared the real or assumed fears of the city corporation that further growth would invite plague and famine. From the year of the Spanish Armada the Crown tried to stop the expansion of London, first by Acts of Parliament, then by proclamations, commissions, and judicial proceedings. The impecunious Charles I, however, at least in the latter part of his reign, used these prohibitions chiefly as a means of raising fines from those who offended against them or bought licences of exemption: by 1638 more than 1,300 houses had been compounded for. The Parliamentary opposition made a grievance of this, but under the Protectorate the same thing went on. In 1661 the futile prohibition was renewed, with the addition of regulations for better building: only stone and brick were permitted.

Overseas expansion and the increase of population at home would have been impossible if there had only been biological changes and better food supply. Many other factors of economic and political organization were necessary to account for them. The colonist depended, though some of them scarcely knew it, on the protection of the State and on the support of capitalists. These factors were also at work in places overseas where there was no question of emigration. Under the Protectorate of Oliver Cromwell the military and naval strength of the State was so great that there was a revival of the old plan of holding bridgehead on the Continent: in 1658 Dunkirk was taken. In this year 1662, however, it was given up on grounds of expense, perhaps a bad thing strategically but economically no loss. In the same year two other possessions were acquired which showed how completely the map of English commerce had changed since the loss of Calais. Both came as parts of the dowry of Charles II's Portuguese queen: the Portuguese empire was hard pressed by the Dutch, and they threw in these two towns as part of the price of the English alliance, by which they saved the rest. The first was Tangier, outside the Straits of Gibraltar on the African shore: its acquisition was a milestone in the progress of English trade and naval power in the Mediterranean. The other was Bombay, our first territorial possession in Asia.

Not only was the realm more populous, and enhanced by these colonies and trading-posts abroad; it had the look of a richer and busier country than in 1572. In the time of Charles I the post office became a national service for carrying letters and packages. There was indeed no great change in inland transport, though new methods had been introduced which were capable of bringing great improvements. Something had been done to improve the rivers, especially the Thames, where pound-locks were constructed. The works were only partly finished, but in the time of James I and Charles I the river was made navigable up to or even beyond Oxford. A number of writers put out projects for other river improvements and for connecting rivers by canals. In the ports there were more visible signs of development. The East India Company had recently completed its dock at Blackwall, the first dock in the Thames in the modern sense of a wet dock with gates. This dock, an acre and a half in extent, was for vessels fitting out after launching: it had no connexion with the landing or shipping of cargoes. The Company had also a dry dock, and there were several others for the repair of ships.

Another comparatively durable part of the nation's equipment consisted of merchant ships. Trade and industries were indeed served as well by foreign as by English-owned ships, and sometimes better; but the English merchant fleet made profits and paid for imports by earning payments for freights. It seems to have grown pretty steadily from the middle of Queen Elizabeth's reign. It is very difficult to compare its size as a whole at different times, because records are scanty and there were many different types of ships. Most of the authorities agree that between 1572 and 1662 the total was more than doubled. It increased considerably between 1572 and the early part of James I's reign. In 1639 the Trinity House even reported that English shipping had increased tenfold in the preceding thirty years. In James I's time there were probably more than 2,000 ships of all sizes, excluding fishing and small craft, of which not less than 400 were over 100 tons, and considerably more than 100 were more than 200 tons.[1] The largest merchant ship the East Indiaman *The Trades Increase* was over 1,000 tons, and, while some of the nearer trades were said to be declining, there was a growing demand for the large ships needed in the American and East India trades. It is clear that England's proportion of the total shipping of Europe had

[1] Figures of tonnage are always ambiguous, and should not be used for exact comparison unless it is known what kind of tons are meant.

increased considerably, though it is not certain whether the Dutch, who still had a far larger merchant marine than the English, had not progressed at an even greater rate. There had been an absolute increase of European shipping, but it was almost wholly made up by the increase of the English and Dutch. The Spaniards and Portuguese had lost ground, the French, Germans, Scots and Italians stayed pretty much as they were.

What we know about agriculture in 1662 agrees with what we know about population and the face of the country; but our knowledge here is scrappy. A good many books advocated agricultural improvement, which suggests an increasing demand for the products of the land; but so far their precepts had not led to any general change of methods. The standard of energy and enlightenment varied a good deal from one part of the country to another. Oliver Cromwell, when he was Protector, said:' I have been in all the counties of England and I think the husbandry of Devonshire is best.' In Devonshire they enriched their land with marl, chalk, lime, sea-sand, compost, soap-ashes, rags, anything that would do it good: perhaps their cloth-making and seafaring neighbours gave them an exceptionally good market. In the more easterly parts of the country the example of the Low Countries pointed to the introduction of new crops, especially new kinds of beans, peas, and 'salads'. It was about this time that asparagus and artichokes came in. Rich men experimented with oranges and lemons in hot-houses, and with new sorts of apples and pears in their orchards. Tobacco was successfully grown in Gloucestershire in the 1650s, but the Government suppressed its cultivation in the interests of the American tobacco colonies. Turnips had been grown as a garden-crop since Queen Elizabeth's time; potatoes came in from America, but they too were still only planted in gardens, not in fields. A royalist exile, the ancestor of Warren Hastings, brought back sainfoin from St. Jean de Luz and grew it successfully at Daylesford in the Cotswolds. Another, Sir Richard Weston introduced clover and other new crops from Flanders and Brabant. They were not economically important yet, but this was another interesting experiment.

Enclosure, the chief method of rural re-organization, seems to have gone on, when market-conditions were favourable, as actively as before. We have even less statistical knowledge for the seventeenth century than for the sixteenth; but all the evidence shows that many open fields were enclosed for pasture, and many for arable. Popular discontent went on through the last years of Queen Elizabeth: there was a feeble attempt at a rising in Oxfordshire in 1596. Corn was very short after the bad harvests of the fifteen-nineties, and 1597 saw another Act against depopulation. It was the last of the series and it was not effective. In 1607 there was trouble in the Midlands: people calling themselves 'Levellers' and 'Diggers' disturbed the peace of Northamptonshire, Warwickshire and Leicestershire. This was followed by a fresh inquiry into depopulation. The Privy Council tried fairly consistently to enforce the law against uncontrolled enclosure, and Archbishop Laud added to his unpopularity by zealously countenancing the commission for depopulation which stood up for the poor against the encroachments of covetous landlords; but he was exceptional among the ministers of Charles I and the Crown itself was active in the most unpopular of all kinds of enclosure, namely draining.

The efforts of the administration do not seem to have had much effect on the economic process of enclosure. The lawyers devised new methods for giving it legal form. When the surveyors had done their work and the parties had reached an agreement for enclosure, they could, by various ingenious forms of procedure, have it ratified by a decree of the Court of Chancery or some other court such as the Duchy Court of Cornwall. This meant trouble and expense, but it meant that the owners had a better title to their new holdings, less open to challenge in the courts by greedy or dissatisfied neighbours. No mere agreement, however, could give so good a title as an Act of Parliament, and in the reign of James I an enclosure in Dorset was carried out by public Act. In the twelve years or so preceding the Civil War and during its course there were complaints from several parts of the country of violent throwing down of enclosure hedges, new and old; yet after the outbreak of war neither Parliament nor the Government ever made any attempt to stay the general process of enclosure. That old policy was dead, though a Bill to set up a more satisfactory procedure for enclosures by commissioners and local juries was rejected in 1653. Another practicable line of conservative reform was to facilitate the better cultivation of the open fields. A majority of the farmers in a parish might be empowered to alter the customs and enforce by-laws against dissentients whose inefficient husbandry spread the weeds and starved the animals; but this policy did not come to anything until rather more than a century later.

The changes in industry were, up to a point, like those in agriculture. If we look at them from the point of view of technology and the rise of comparatively large industrial units, we may indeed say that the country had become more industrialized. The output of coal had increased enormously. Here we have some statistics, but they are more difficult to interpret than is commonly supposed, and we must not be too confident in asserting that the increase was in the region of eight- or tenfold. Perhaps the whole kingdom was producing some two million tons a year. The main source of supply was the north-east, and the monopoly of the Newcastle 'hostmen' was a highly developed industrial combination. Most of the 'sea-coal' shipped to London and the east Midlands was for domestic fuel, but perhaps a third of the whole output was used in industry, though as yet only for heat and not for power. Coal was taking the place of wood and charcoal as timber became scarce and dear; but some of the industries which used fuel were themselves growing. Iron was coming to be smelted in blast furnaces; there was more work for smiths; probably more lime was burnt.

There is an interesting group of industries, some new and some old, in which coal was probably indispensable for production on the scale now needed. The salt-pans which were started round Berwick and elsewhere in the sixteenth century; the dye-houses; the London breweries, some of which worked for export, used coal. So did the sugar refineries. Coke was used in malting in James I's time, as earlier in Germany. Soap-boiling was a new or at least a much improved trade of the same period, also introduced from the Continent. One of the great industrial events of Elizabeth's reign was the discovery of alum in the Isle of Wight and in Yorkshire: the equipment for working it cost thousands of pounds, but, with royal protection against imports, some of the richest men of the time made their fortunes in this industry. It was the alum monopoly that paid for Sir Arthur Ingram's palace at Temple Newsam. Saltpetre was extracted, with the use of fuel, from unsavoury deposits in stables and elsewhere: the growth of the gunpowder industry made this business important until it was superseded by imports from India in the time of Charles I. The Venetian Giacomo Verzellini, who made exquisite glasses under a patent granted by Queen Elizabeth in 1575, had no successors, but glass-making of humbler kinds was established at or about the time we are speaking of. Coal was also coming into use in brickfields, pot-banks, and tile-works, in all of which some degree of invention or contrivance was needed for the purpose.

These are not the only examples of technological improvement and the introduction of new trades. In the great woollen industry, the spinning-wheel had almost completed its victory over the rock or distaff, and the Saxony wheel, an improved type which spun two threads at once, was coming into use. There was now a definitely established cotton industry in Lancashire. The most complicated machine used in any industry at this time was the stocking-frame or knitting-machine. It was an English invention, the first great technological invention for which the nation can claim the credit, and it was made, towards the end of Elizabeth's reign, not by a mere artificer, but by a Cambridge graduate. Its home was in the counties of Nottingham, Derby and Leicester. By 1662 it too had been improved: it could now be managed by one worker instead of two. It was much more expensive than an ordinary loom, and so those who owned stocking-frames tended to be rather capitalists than craftsmen, and the making of them led to a fresh division of labour. But we must be careful not to misunderstand these changes in technology. They had not yet widely altered the relations of capital and labour, nor even the total national output of goods. There were only 600 stocking-frames in the whole country in 1660. And in some other instances a list of places where a new trade was established gives a very misleading impression. There are records of many paper-mills set up, some of them with foreign work-men, from Tudor times onwards; but a well-informed book in this very year 1662 said that then no paper was made in England.

In spite of their technical progress, the metal trades did not all flourish. Lead-mining was thriving more about this time than ever before, and the zinc from the Mendips had started in Bristol and elsewhere the first English manufacture of brass. For the present the yellow metal industry had only a modest output of small utensils, and much of the calamine was illegally shipped abroad, for Sweden was the great source of copper. Moreover, as brass rose, pewter went down, so the new activity was not all clear gain for the nation. As a whole, however, the metal industries were rising. The great wars, from the Armada to the Civil War, brought a demand for bullets, for cannon and for the metal parts of small arms and vehicles. In the intervals of peace the iron-founders of the Weald succeeded in finding other uses for their mills, such as making the well-known Sussex fire-backs. In 1662 a wire-mill

was set up by a Dutchman or German at Sheen, near
Richmond.

The advance of industry was remarkable. It was not
out of all proportion to the growth of population and
the development of agriculture; but these three sets
of changes are not enough to explain one another.
For a full explanation, perhaps of the other two and
certainly of the industrial changes, we must look
outside them—that is, to the state of commerce. Here
we find the greatest of all the contrasts between the
England of 1572 and of 1662. Seaborne commerce
had, to all appearance, grown in volume; though we
cannot say how much, and in all probability it had
grown proportionately less than industry. In other
words, the increased population and the increase of
consumption per head, if such there was, had been
provided for more by home production than by
exports; the amount of foreign trade per head of
population was probably less, not more. All this is,
however, uncertain. Where we reach plain facts is in
the commodities and geography of commerce. In the
range of commodities there was no very great change.
The woollen manufactures were still the predominant
goods for export. Probably they were less so than
before; they accounted now for about two-thirds of the
total. Some raw wool was still exported, though
attempts were now made to enforce medieval laws
prohibiting the export. Equally illegal, though not
negligible in value, were the exports of alum, copperas,
and fuller's earth. Coal exports had grown to somewhere in the region of 100,000 tons. The only other
great change in the export trade was the beginning of
the re-exporting of goods brought from great distances,

especially pepper, spices and cotton-goods from the East, tobacco and sugar from America. The list of imports was, as of old, long and miscellaneous; it was in fact longer and more miscellaneous than ever. The main supply of saltpetre now came from India, which was also sending indigo. Logwood, another dyeing material, was coming in from the Bay of Honduras and the Mosquito Coast.

In the geography of English commerce there had been a greater change than in any other century of our history. The old close connexion with the Low Countries and the old dependent status of England as the new country were gone and even forgotten. With the blockading and fall of Antwerp, the textile industry of Flanders and Brabant had lost its main outlet and its European primacy, and so, on the one hand, left the way open for the rise of English textile exports and, on the other, ceased to take off English half-finished goods. The Merchant Adventurers moved their staple to various places, and in 1598 settled at Middelburg in Dutch territory. Other centres of industry had their opportunity just as the English had, among them the industry of the free Netherlands, centred on Leyden. In 1613 King James I had taken up the project of Alderman Cokayne, who intended to organize the export of finished cloth on a great scale, and so induced the King to revoke the privileges of the Merchant Adventurers. The project ended disastrously; it was a wild-cat scheme; and the worst of the disaster was that the States of Holland took retaliatory measures which ushered in a long period, not ended in 1662, of commercial hostilities. By 1662 the whole English commerce with the two halves of the Netherlands, Spanish and free, so far from predominating, was only one of half a dozen trades of the same order of magnitude. The economic centre of the Netherlands had shifted to the north: Amsterdam was now the greatest port of western Europe and the greatest money-market; but our relation to Amsterdam was the opposite of our old relation to Antwerp. Instead of being mutually dependent and complementary, we and the Dutch were rivals. The Dutch were more advanced in their commercial methods; in some parts of the world we had difficulty in competing with them; in some we could scarcely even maintain a foothold; but everywhere our rivalry with them was the main concern of our most active traders. Ours, like theirs, was now a developed country, drawing raw materials from the new countries and selling manufactured articles to them, earning profits from shipping, and by 'conscious imitation of the Dutch' emancipating itself from the last trammels of dependence. English ships still had to be insured in Amsterdam; the Dutch had the trade of Russia almost entirely in their own hands, and we had as yet made little headway against them in acquiring a share of the Hanseatic inheritance in Scandinavia and the Baltic; but all over the world the contest was at its height. In 1662 the first Anglo-Dutch war was only a few years past, and another was evidently brewing.

In this transitional state of European commerce one of our largest single trades was with France, from which we imported wines, silks, and other textiles to a considerably greater value than the exports which France was able to absorb from us. The imports from France were finished products and luxuries, so France was not helping us to establish our position as a fully developed country. We now had a great Mediterranean trade, perhaps larger altogether than our French trade. In the Levant there was a market for our manufactures and the 'returns' were mostly food and raw materials; but here France, especially Marseilles, was a skilful and experienced competitor. Not far below the French and Mediterranean trades was that with Spain, including trade through Spain to the Spanish colonies. Nominally, we had no direct trade with the Spanish colonies, but in fact we smuggled a good deal; and all this Spanish trade took off our finished products in exchange for wines and for primary products which gave employment here. There was a similar but much smaller trade with Portugal and the Portuguese dependencies. In 1661 a treaty was made with Portugal confirming that of 1654 in which Oliver Cromwell had established a close economic connexion with Portugal. These treaties opened direct trade with Brazil and the Portuguese stations in West Africa, and we imported sugar, refined and unrefined, from Brazil, partly for re-export.

Our commercial relations with every one of the more important European countries were thus inextricably mixed with our commerce outside Europe, and the greatest of all the changes in our trade was the rise of our trade with the East and with America. The East India company, founded in direct competition with the Dutch, though still far smaller than the Dutch company, was the greatest of English commercial institutions. Its assets were worth about £500,000. It had factories on the Persian Gulf, in India, in Java and Sumatra. Their prospects were indeed uncertain. The Persian trade was in a bad way. Envious merchants at home set on economists to criticize the company for failing to export home products and for making up the deficiency by carrying bullion out of the realm. The expedition which started in 1662 to take possession of Bombay did not expect to have an easy task. Above all, there was the hostility of the Dutch. They had not handed over the spice island of Run in the Malay Archipelago, which belonged by treaty to the English company. They had seized ships. There was a long account to settle with them. But English ships were at work bringing Eastern goods, salt-petre, indigo, pepper, spices, cotton piece-goods, to London.

The American trade was not in the hands of a company, but of many firms of moderate size. In total quantity it was probably not far different from the trade with the East Indies or Holland or France. Its structure was complex, or rather it consisted of various separate parts which were now being drawn together into a complex whole. In relation to the American colonies, England was, more clearly than anywhere else, the old country dealing with new countries. The West Indian islands were booming. They sent tobacco and increasing quantities of unrefined sugar for the refineries of Bristol. The northern colonies, which lived by mixed farming, had a difficulty in finding return cargoes to pay for their imports of manufactured articles; but they were looking for commercial opportunities. In America too there was international rivalry. Some of the plantations were still financed by Dutch capital. Some of the islands were still dependent on Dutch shipping. In 1662 Charles II granted a charter to the Royal African Company, which was intended to take out of the hands of the Dutch the profitable business of supplying the colonies with negro slaves.

Here we must notice the course of the general history of prices. The price revolution continued to affect English economy for some time after 1572 in the same way as before. The English, like the French, were able to sell at a great profit to the countries where its effects were more intense. They thus obtained silver which they used to immense advantage by re-exporting it to the East. But about the middle of the seventeenth century the price revolution had run its course. The imports of treasure into Spain showed a marked decline in the first thirty years of the seventeenth century and in the next thirty a precipitate drop. For this there were no doubt many causes, such as an increase of smuggling to other countries, a rise in the expense of mining, a decrease in the fertility of the mines, changes in monetary policy, increases in the internal trade of the Spanish West Indies and of their direct trade with Asia. Whatever the reasons, the graph of Spanish prices which had been rising for a century now ran level or actually declined. In most of the countries of Europe the same change came about, after a longer or shorter interval of time, and in England the general level of prices steadied down by about 1650. England therefore had to contend, like the neighbouring nations, with economic problems far different from those of the long and fruitful inflation. There were indeed considerable oscillations of prices, cyclical changes like those we have already mentioned; and there was perhaps still some slight general rise; but the great expansive phase was over. The change was most marked in the prices of industrial products, so that industry suffered more than agriculture from the restriction, and made matters worse by price-cutting. The new phase was favourable to creditors against debtors, and so it presented the governments with budgetary and monetary problems. As the debtors found it hard to pay and funds were scarce, financiers restricted their credits, so that purchasing power was diminished. Intense competition for customers arose between and within the nations. Every business man who could do so reduced his costs by mechanization or rationalization; this added to the unemployment caused by lack of demand, and therefore still further reduced the consumers' demand. It seemed that no one could prosper except at the expense of some direct or indirect competitor.

Down to about 1572 the prices of the chief western European countries had moved pretty well in unison; but after that date those of some countries diverge from those of others. This shows that the structure of international trade and finance was impaired; there was a less free flow of money and goods. We know in fact that this was so. The great age of Antwerp had ended. Minor international markets like Lyons also sank into insignificance about the same time. There followed a struggle for the succession, and Amsterdam was becoming the chief candidate at about the time when the Thirty Years War of 1618–48 began to handicap first the German cities and then the French. These vicissitudes of the international structure were reflected in the contrasts between the prices of various groups of commodities in England. Spices were cheaper or dearer according to the success or failure of the English to win a share in this trade which had slipped from the hands of the Portuguese. Metals and textiles continued to rise in price longer than other commodities, perhaps because of the foreign demand for munitions of war and the opening up of new markets for woollens abroad; but building materials for which there was no important export market began to fall as early as the sixteen-thirties, while cattle, horses and animal products reached their maximum in the sixteen-forties, cereal and vegetable products about the middle of the century.

CHAPTER V

BRITAIN AFTER THE PRICE REVOLUTION, TO 1662

How had these considerable economic changes affected the composition and relations of the different social strata? They had kept the lines of demarcation fluid, possibly made them even more fluid: when there were so many ways of making and losing money, the lucky and the ambitious went up while the improvident or unfortunate went down. The richest men did not live now very differently from the richest men of Elizabeth's time. A man of some ability, Thomas Wilson, who had access to the official papers of his uncle and namesake, the writer on usury, wrote a description of England in 1600 in which he estimated the numbers and average incomes of the various classes. We ought not to take his figures too seriously, but they are worth noting. He gives figures of the revenues of various classes in the late Elizabethan days. The richest peer, the Earl of Oxford, was rated at £12,000 for taxation in 1575 and squandered all he had; the rest of the peers had incomes running down to less than £3,000. The bishoprics varied from between £2,000 and £3,000 to less than £500. The value of Church lands could not be estimated from the rents, since the clergy usually did not rack-rent, but reserved part of their rents in kind. Besides some inferior people who had been knighted there were about 500 knights who lived as they should, with between £1,000 and £2,000 a year, but a few had anything up to £7,000. The squires, with £500 to £1,000 rent, numbered about

16,000, of whom 1,400 were in the commission of the peace. In the North a gentleman of good reputation might be content with £300 or £400. The pestilent lawyers might make enormous incomes: Sir Edward Coke, the Attorney-General, who less than ten years earlier had not had £100 a year, now had between £12,000 and £14,000. There were accounted to be 10,000 rich yeomen, with anything up to £300 or £500 a year, who could give their daughters marriage portions of £1,000. This class, however, was decaying. There were 80,000 freeholders worth £300 or £500 in stock.

Less than a generation later we find still greater fortunes. At the outbreak of the Civil War the Earl of Worcester was said to have a revenue of £24,000, and the peerage generally had money incomes perhaps twice as high as in 1572 in pounds sterling. At the death of Elizabeth there were fifty-nine lay peers; at the death of James I about 100, at the Restoration, 142; so that, even if the rise in their money incomes was mainly accounted for by the fall in the value of money, at any rate the country was supporting more of them. Of those newly created, a good many may be described as statesmen, courtiers, and landed magnates; there were a few judges and soldiers; but there was a number of merchants who went straight to the House of Lords without a generation or two to qualify them as landowners. The city alliances of the peerage were, however, more frequent and more splendid than before. Seven of the children of Alderman Cokayne married into noble families. Charles I gave peerages to three business men, Sir Paul Bayning, Baptist Hicks, who became Viscount Campden, and William Craven.

By this time it was evident that most of the richest men in the country were City men. Even in Norwich Thomas Wilson had known twenty-four aldermen who were esteemed to be worth £20,000 apiece. In London some were worth £100,000 and a man was not esteemed rich unless he had £50,000. Many of them were absorbed into the governing class as it already existed, the richest into the nobility, the merely rich into the gentry. There were indeed many substantial traders and professional men who did not buy farms or set up as squires, but contented themselves with a career in the City companies and corporation, and with their mansions or suburban gardens. The City had its own pride and consciousness, and played a great part in national affairs; but it did not develop an urban patriciate like those of the great commercial cities of the Continent. Still less did any such class emerge in the provincial towns.

Between 1572 and 1662 there had occurred the greatest upheaval that England has known since the twelfth century, the 'Puritan' Revolution. The story of these events has often been told in political, constitutional, and ecclesiastical terms; but no one doubts nowadays that they were also events in economic history. Historians do not, however, agree about their economic aspects. The Civil War had some of the economic effects which, as we have seen, were common to all wars. Perhaps because there were important business men on the Parliamentary side, it marked an advance in the applications of capitalism to war. The Parliamentary authorities made considerable bulk purchases of clothing, boots, and weapons, larger than any single orders that had ever been given before in England. After the Restoration there were for some time no more such centralized contracts, and each regiment had to clothe and equip itself out of the soldier's pay. This wave of economic stimulation rose and subsided again, and the same is true of some other striking economic changes of the time.

The disturbances cleared the way for some permanent changes. In public finance both sides experimented with forms of taxation, which, after short periods of uncertainty, were afterwards made permanent. There was the excise, copied from the Dutch, a tax on sales of certain commodities at home. There were new direct taxes, especially apportioned taxes on landowners. The taxes were modernized because large sums were needed and the old tenths and fifteenths and subsidies were too erratic in their incidence to be worth adapting for the purpose. Thus there were some temporary and some permanent economic changes; yet in many directions there was no change at all. Just as the machinery of justice, the courts and law officers, went on working without interruption except for a few months, so the development of the rules of law by judicial decisions went on. There was much agitation for law reform, but not even in the most revolutionary phases of the crisis was there any important legislation in the land law or commercial law or the law of contracts.

These contrasts between change and continuity can be explained from the social aspect of the crisis. It began in the last years of Elizabeth and developed in the reigns of James I and Charles I through differences between the Crown and Parliament. From the time of James I there was an opposition party which had a religious programme and was ambitious to increase the power of Parliament. Its chief lever was the power of taxation, and it resisted the attempts of the Crown to raise money by extra-Parliamentary means. Some of these, like the revival of the forest law and the revival of knighthood fines on the old standard, were oppressive; but the opposition objected to them all for the further reason that if they had succeeded they would have made the Crown independent. Parliament had its centre of gravity in the newly consolidated circle of the gentry. The leaders of the discontented party gained support from business men, often closely associated with them in joint-stock enterprises, who objected to this or that article of commercial policy, such as monopolies, the arbitrary manipulation of Customs rates, and the other alleged causes, whatever they might be, of commercial depressions. When it came to open war, these gentlemen and the minority of the nobility who were with them were victorious, partly because of the wealth and organizing capacity of their side, partly because of sea-power, which meant very much the same thing, but partly also because of the force of Puritan conviction which inspired the extremist minority. They armed a large part of the populace, and the soldiers were full of ideas, all the revolutionary ideas which had been stirred up in the sixteenth century by the Reformation. For years it was impossible to agree on a peace-settlement, and during these years the Army, with no fighting to do, but cheated of its pay, remembered the ancient grievances of the populace from which it had been recruited. In the end the Levellers in the Army were put down. So were the handful of Diggers, the civilian followers of Gerald Winstanley, who took possession of a piece of waste land near Walton-on-Thames intending to cultivate it on communist principles.

Power was for a few years in the hands of Oliver Cromwell and his supporters, some of them gentlemen born, some newly risen in the Civil War. Their social policy was conservative, and all hopes of social revolution were vain even before the final convulsions which restored Charles II.

The twenty years of crisis left their mark on the social structure of the country. In the first place, they continued to feed the real estate market as it had been fed by the sales of the Tudor monarchs. Queen Elizabeth by the end of her reign had sold land to the amount of £807,000. James I and Charles I, unable to get adequate financial support from Parliament, went on with the process to the tune of £1,425,000. After the outbreak of civil war, both sides, to supply their financial needs, confiscated and sold the estates of their opponents; but the winning side were naturally able to do this on a far greater scale than the losers, whose sales were soon invalidated. Parliament raised nearly £2,000,000 by sales of Crown lands, and after that it sold the estates of the bishops, deans, and chapters. Parts of the lands of individual royalists were confiscated and other parts sold by the owners to pay taxes and fines. At the Restoration most of these transferences were annulled, but purchasers who had paid good money for the estates of individual royalists were not dispossessed, so that there was a fairly large permanent residue of new owners, reinforced by those who had made money out of the troubles. At the same time, very large transactions in Irish confiscated land were going on, so that great sums of money, mobilized in large part by rich operators from commerce, industry, and savings, were changing hands. This continued activity of the market does not, however,

appear to have had the same effect on the gentry
as the earlier activity. As a body, the gentry reached
their highest point about the time of the Civil War.
After that there is no evidence that their consolidation
went further. Not only were the disturbances adverse
for individuals, such as those Royalists who were not
restored to their estates; the gentry as a whole were
less prominent than the merchants and financiers
among the ultimate purchasers. They no longer had
much surplus to invest.

Like those of earlier times, these transferences of
land often increased the inducements to strict commercial management of estates. So long as the government had the sequestrated lands in hand, it had a good
reason for extracting all they would yield. Many
private persons did likewise. We do not know how
widely this happened. Easy-going landlords still
survived side by side with extortioners; in the regions
where this matter has been closely examined there
seems to be a patchwork which only the chances of
personality could explain in detail. Nor have we any
figures for the amount of poverty and unemployment,
except the rough outline of the relation between wages
and the cost of living. This seems to indicate that
some few years before the outbreak of the Civil War
food was dearer than ever before and wages were not
keeping up with this rise. As the proportion of people
mainly dependent on wages was also growing, this
was serious. It must have had something to do with
the gravity of the political crisis. As the crisis went
from bad to worse wheat prices and prices in general
fell, and the position of the poor man was easier.

Beyond that unfortunately little can be said about the
poor in this period. As to the legal 'poor', we know

much about the legislation for them. In Queen Elizabeth's reign the poor law was consolidated, and a great Act of 1601 completed the main lines of its development. The most important subsequent change was made by an Act of 1662, which made a number of improvements and defined the law of settlement. Since the deserving poor were entitled to relief, it was someone's duty to give it; but it could not be the duty of every parish to relieve every pauper, wherever he came from. London and Westminster already attracted swarms of vagabonds from all over the country, and the same thing might happen elsewhere. Each man or woman was entitled to relief only where he had a settlement, where he belonged. The Act of 1662 gave justices of the peace the power to remove paupers compulsorily from places where they had no settlement. This was a check to the mobility of labour, but only to mobility under the least desirable of all conditions, the forced and perhaps purposeless flight of the destitute. This part of the law was sometimes enforced harshly.

We know a good deal about how the poor law was administered. Under the Stuart kings the Privy Council kept a sharp eye on the local authorities, except in the North, Devon, Cornwall, Wiltshire, and Wales (afterwards the centres of royalism), where the law was administered carelessly if at all. During the eleven years when Charles I governed without a Parliament, his Privy Council made a vigorous effort to see that the local authorities relieved even the widespread poverty caused by trade depressions; but unfortunately we do not know how far they succeeded. The best things done under the law were, however, due to the initiative of the local authorities, especially

n some of the boroughs. They experimented in
providing work for the unemployed and relief for
the helpless, sometimes doing more than the law
equired of them and occasionally even more than it
permitted. The confusion of the central administration
n the war and the interregnum did not cause a break-
down in the poor law, and perhaps made little differ-
nce. Finance, the mainspring, was entirely local. For
hat reason we know little about the economic history
f the poor law. We cannot even guess at the total
mount raised in rates, at the numbers relieved in the
ountry as a whole or even at the upward and down-
ward fluctuations of their numbers. We cannot decide
whether the poor law aided the changes in agriculture
nd industry. Very likely it did, for it provided a third
means of livelihood, neither peasant self-support, nor
wage-labour, but parish relief.

The economic writings of the period and the
Parliamentary speeches on economic matters are
oncrete and practical. When they take up a theo-
etical point, they still do not follow it very far, and
hey do not imply much knowledge of business
rganization outside the circles of those who worked
n it. They nearly all have the pessimistic and defensive
ote that we might expect in a period of rapid change.
n the latter part of Queen Elizabeth's time Sir Walter
Raleigh and others advocated colonization as a remedy
or the excess of population at home, and in 1662 it was
omething of a paradox for Sir William Petty to
maintain that the country needed not lands, but hands.
A new tendency of the time had been the beginning
f various lines of thought that look to an incautious
modern reader like 'economic liberalism'. A number

of different kinds of restraint on trade hampered the enterprising business men, and so they, or the writer they hired, when they protested in Parliament or outside it against these specific restrictions, often expressed themselves in phrases that might easily have a wide application. Thus in 1604 there was a Parliamentary attack on the privileges of trading companies in the course of which many phrases about liberty were used and a Bill was drafted which was called a Bill for free trade. In 1623 an author writing on behalf of the East India Company used the phrase 'natural liberty' in connexion with trade. These people, and others like them, seemed to be invoking general principles; but they had not worked these principles out and deliberately adopted them. They merely expressed without consideration a principle towards which their particular views or interests tended.

Interests were claiming attention which did indeed tend towards the relaxation of State control. First and by far the most important among them, was the opposition to monopolies. Queen Elizabeth granted a number of monopolies to projectors who introduced or promised to introduce, new trades. We have already noticed those which were of real value. Since, however the Crown took a payment for each of these grants, the Queen gave others, equally remunerative to the Crown, but merely burdensome to the nation. The ancient tin industry was subjected to one, the making of playing-cards to another; altogether there were many of them, and they were given, not to business men, but to people whom historians picturesquely describe as 'courtiers'. Elizabeth's last Parliament protested angrily, and the Queen in person in a 'golden speech' promised to submit all the monopolies to the scrutiny of the courts of law. The common law against restraint of trade proved an uncertain safeguard and in 1621 James I gave his assent to the Statute of Monopolies, which limited the grants of monopoly by royal letters patent to special cases for which there seemed to be an economic justification. The first great class of exceptions was formed by the charters of companies; the second was that to which we give the name 'patent' in ordinary speech, grants to those who invented or introduced new processes. The great collection of specifications in the Patent Office begins from this time. Even this settlement did not end the trouble; Charles I, in his efforts to raise money, strained this law; but in its general lines it lasted. The controversy left behind it a shrewd suspicion among business men that State control might easily do them more harm than good.

When they were in difficulties, the business men still appealed to the State for help, and the help they asked for was usually some form of State control. The two interests most affected by crises were the woollen manufacture and finance. The woollen manufacture depended on a foreign market, and so it suffered both from foreign competition and from the wars and other misfortunes which made transport dangerous or impoverished the buyers. No one thought of remedying this by international agreements; that would indeed have been impracticable. Pessimists in times of depression urged that England suffered from 'overmuch drapery'. They did not, however, suggest any way of promoting a more balanced economy by raising the level of other industries; all they could do was to make plans for restricting the scale and regulating the quality of the staple manufacture. Thus in 1640

E

a royal commission proposed that exclusive corporations should be established in the clothing towns on the model of the Colchester Corporation for bays. Each was to have control within a radius of six, ten, or fourteen miles round about. Altogether there were to be sixty-one of them, and we may pause for a moment to look at the map of the clothing industry as this plan reveals it. East Anglia was to have eleven corporations, Wiltshire five, Dorset two, Hampshire three, Somerset six, Devon five, Gloucestershire and the Cotswolds four, Worcestershire two, Berkshire two, Surrey one (at Guildford), Shropshire two, then there were to be three in Kent and one at Coventry, while Staffordshire was to have two. North of the Trent there were to be six in Lancashire and five in the West Riding of Yorkshire, with an outlying corporation at Kendal in Westmorland. They would not all have been equally important, but these numbers tell us something about the shifting of business from one region to another. Wiltshire and the Cotswolds were having a bad time. East Anglia was doing better, but the North was competing for first place.

Nothing came of this plan, mainly because it was made on the eve of the Civil War. In any case, although it was a scheme for control, it was not a plan for direct State control, and it was meant to end the vexatious system by which royal officers, the aulnagers, had enforced regulations of quality mainly as a means of raising revenue. The system of corporations still had life in it. New charters were given to craft guilds in some of the towns, and some of them were important. In 1624 the Sheffield cutlers got their Company by Act of Parliament. In 1650 the Norwich weavers got their corporation; in 1657 the framework knitters were incorporated; and these were not all. Some of the new foundations were associations of substantial capitalists, and there were fresh instances of the amalgamation of companies by which they came under oligarchical control. This had begun, as we saw, in London; now it happened in the provinces: in 1574 at Northampton, for instance, in 1616 at Faversham, in 1622 at Norwich, in the next year at Lichfield. The old corporative system did not, however, adapt itself sufficiently to the increased size and expansiveness of business. Most of the old guilds clung to their little local monopolies and became the strongholds of municipal resistance to the rise of the individual capitalist. Amalgamations now represented a common effort at defence; but the enemy was strong. The new industries grew up outside the hedges of the Tudor code. Parliament had to deal with labour problems too great for the old compartments. In 1660 it was urgently necessary to resettle a horde of disbanded soldiers in civil life, and so they were allowed to practise trades without regard to the old rules about apprenticeship and entry. From this side too the tide had set in the direction of relieving industry from legal restraints.

The sphere in which the State could intervene most effectively was that of foreign commerce, and here there was a new reason for intervention. In the first phase of the seventeenth century there were some experiments in lightening the burdens on commerce, including an attempt to make Dover into something like a 'free port'. When the great price revolution ended, the states behaved as competitors always behave in times of depression, and a new phase of protectionism and trade wars set in. An Act of 1650, which probably had little practical effect, denied to foreign ships the right to trade with the English colonies. The famous Navigation Act of the following year was aimed at the Dutch. It was meant to exclude them from some very profitable branches of commerce. With some exceptions it prohibited the importation into the territory of the Commonwealth of any kind of goods except in English ships or the ships of the country in which the goods originated, It applied whether the country of origin was in or out of Europe, British or foreign, so it shut English ports to any foreign merchant bringing Colonial goods or European re-exports. This law was not the main cause of the first Dutch war, but in their declaration of war the Dutch mentioned it as an unfriendly act. The British victory in the war made it impossible for the Dutch to demand its repeal, and the British interests which benefited under the Act, the shipbuilders and the East and West India merchants, overcame the opposition of those who would have profited if the Dutch had still been allowed to sell us their ships and to carry supplies to the colonies. From the beginning some licences were granted to act in contravention of this law and some traders contravened it without licences, but at the Restoration it was renewed. It was not merely re-enacted. It was supplemented by protective tariff provisions, and it was extended to include the terms of the Act of 1650. From 1660 no supplies were to be carried to the English plantations except in English ships or those of the plantations themselves; there were to be no foreign factors or agents in the plantations. Certain very important plantation goods, 'the enumerated commodities'—sugar, tobacco, raw cotton, indigo and other dyestuffs—were to be shipped only to English ports. England was to become a staple for these goods as Amsterdam was for East India goods. The mutual dependence of the old country and its new suppliers of primary products was to be organized so as to exclude third parties. And it was not only against the Dutch that English protectionism was defined. The French, as yet less powerful rivals in seaborne trade, were also excluded like the rest of the world. In 1648 for a political reason, the importation of English draperies was prohibited in most of France. As a reprisal, Parliament prohibited the importing of French wine and woollen and silk goods. Again in 1654, the French increased their duties on British cloth and, in 1659, they laid a new duty on foreign tonnage in their ports.

In all this there was no new principle. The states were indeed becoming better able to control the innumerable smugglers who evaded these regulations, and protectionism was becoming better able to open or shut the gateways to the realm and its dependencies. But the greater economic experience of the seventeenth century and the greater pressure of international competition cleared the way for some new ideas which were already clearly expressed, though they had not yet brought about large practical results. The first was the idea that science should be applied to economic development. The great scientific movement which transformed European thought in the seventeenth century had a utilitarian side, and some of the best English scientists hoped that their investigations would be useful for the working of mines and for improving the processes of manufactures. In 1662 King Charles II gave his charter to the Royal Society, his purpose being 'to promote the welfare of the arts', the useful arts, as well as the sciences. Very wide horizons were opening. In this same year John Graunt published his *Observations upon the Bills of Mortality*, the first serious contribution to the statistical study of population. He had the assistance of Sir William Petty, a man who both in theory and in practice embodied the conviction that exact scientific study, if possible on the basis of figures, is the best approach alike to technology and to social policy.

Throughout the period powerful groups of capitalists, acting under charters from the Crown, were organizing the new commerce and the new industry in companies. For branches of commerce where it was easy to find sufficient capital the old form of the regulated company, similar to the Staplers and Merchant Adventurers, was adequate, and new companies on this model were incorporated for Spain and Portugal (1577), the Eastland—that is, the countries bordering on the Baltic (1579)—and France (1611). The Levant Company, originating as a joint-stock company in 1581, became a regulated company in 1600. These London companies had to contend, not only with the hindrances to trade in foreign parts, but also with the opposition of the provincial 'outports', so that by 1662 the French company and the Spanish company were extinct. The same fate for one reason or another overtook a number of joint-stock companies too; but joint stock had definitely established itself as the best method for large enterprises where common action in the markets or in organizing production was profitable. This was evidently the case in the distant foreign trades, so besides some short-lived companies for other trades, the great East India Company was founded in 1601. Colonization was another obvious field for joint stock, and in the period of the great migration it was used for Virginia, Bermuda, Massachusetts, for other places in America, for Ulster, and for the English fens. An ambitious fishery company founded in 1661 was the third in that field. In the seventeenth century the application of joint stock to mining was extended to coal and iron, though as yet on a small scale; in the salt and saltpetre industries it was used, though not with much success. In 1662, in fact, it looked as if the great individual entrepreneurs were the best exploiters of mines, like William Blackett who was becoming powerful on Tyneside.

As the companies multiplied their finance became more skilful and the market for stocks and shares developed. As yet, however, it was far behind that of Amsterdam, and indeed English finance in general, both public and private, had not changed much since Tudor times. There were no banks owned by public authorities or acting under their auspices; banking was a branch of individual trade, except that the State sometimes compelled corporations to lend it money, as James I compelled the City to finance the settlement of Londonderry and Oliver, the Protector, took loans from the East India Company. The root of the troubles of the Stuart kings was that after the price revolution their old hereditary revenues were not enough to pay their necessary expenses. James I was said to have half the ordinary revenue of the grand duke of Tuscany. The experiments of the interregnum had pointed the way to improvements of taxation, and at the Restoration Parliament, wishing the king well, to put his revenue on a satisfactory footing, guaranteeing him an annual income of £1,200,000. It was, however, already clear that this arrangement had been based on inadequate calculation both of the yield of taxes and of the expenditure that would be required, and the King was likely to go short again. The reform of finance was still an urgent need.

In one respect public finance was modernized at the Restoration. Part of James I's income came from the 'incidents' of tenures in capite, miscellaneous dues which the King raised from his tenants on certain chance occasions, such as the minority of a tenant or the knighting of the heir to the throne. They were difficult to collect and irritating to the payers, so James proposed that Parliament should commute them for a fixed annual tax. They failed to agree on the price; but during the interregnum these dues were allowed to lapse, and Charles II's ministers wished neither to revive them nor to collect the arrears. The King was compensated by a hereditary excise, amounting to £100,000 a year, on beer. There was an outcry. A tax on the consumption of all classes had been substituted for a payment by a small number of men of property. It is, however, an error to say that landed property had been exempted from taxation. The change affected only those landlords who held direct from the King, and when it was made they, in common with all other landlords, were paying a stiff 'monthly assessment', one of the new direct taxes introduced by Parliament under the year 1644, during the Civil War, and continued from then until after the Restoration.

We may conclude our survey of the history down to 1662 by very briefly reviewing the fluctuations of trade and finance since 1572. Some of the crises have been mentioned already. From about 1575 there were eleven good years; but in 1586-7 there was a crisis followed by seventeen years of sinking or at least violently fluctuating business, beginning with the Armada year and going on through the very bad harvests of the fifteen-nineties to famine and crisis in 1595-8, and again to plague and crisis in 1603. The 'free trade' agitation of 1603 petered out in the beginning of a prosperous phase, and except for the cloth-trade disaster in 1616-17 caused by Cokayne's project, things went well until 1620. From then until Charles I came to the throne in 1625 was a bad time: Germany was deep in the Thirty Years War, the cloth trade had not recovered, trade was unsatisfactory in the East Indies and Russia, harvests were bad. Except for a revival in 1626-8, and for progress in the Mediterranean and some other trades, these and similar misfortunes went on through Charles's reign, the period of emigration, until the Civil War plunged everything into depression. After something of a recovery about 1650 there came the strain and losses of the first Dutch war, and then a brief period of rather better trade in 1655-7, followed by the Spanish war and another depression in the cloth trade. The year 1659 saw Europe pacified after a long war between France and Spain, so that the Restoration of Charles II came at a happy moment and in 1662 the economic sky was still brighter than it had been for a generation.

The fluctuations were, after all, only waves on the surface of a rising tide, and in some ways they even brought advantages with them. When trade was bad prices were low, and this was good for the consumers. In some of the depressed periods money which could not be profitably invested in trade was put, to the permanent advantage of the country, into solid buildings. Diet was becoming more varied and more rational. There were still occasional years of famine; such were 1630–7, 1645–51, and 1658–61; but there were now fresh resources to fall back on. From the middle of the century rice was imported. The growing quantities of sugar brought with them the custom of eating fruit tarts and puddings after meat courses. The development of England had its good effects: people were eating more butter and cheese. Butter and green vegetables were still despised as the poor man's food, but the dairymen and market gardeners round London were thriving as this prejudice died away. When medical authorities first discussed rickets, from 1645, it was common both in England and in Ireland, so that there was evidently need for a greater use of protective foods; the connexion of rickets with diet was unknown; and it was a mere happy chance that the nation cured itself by eating greens. In drink too there were changes: in 1638 the London Distillers' Company was incorporated.

CHAPTER VI

BRITAIN DURING THE INDUSTRIAL REVOLUTION, TO 1760

THE year 1760 was a war year. There was a stir in the munition industries. In the previous year the first State-owned powder factory had been set up at Faversham, and John Guest, from Shropshire, had become manager of a new company formed to develop the ironworks of Dowlais in Glamorgan; on New Year's Day this year the first furnace was blown at the famous Carron Ironworks in Stirlingshire. Ship-wrights, weavers, horse-breeders, farmers were hard at work for the fleet and the armies. It may seem inappropriate to make our fourth survey at such a point; it may seem that a year of peace would be more normal in the strict sense of the word, more suitable as a standard for comparison with other years. But the wars of the eighteenth century, each greater than the last, did even more than the wars of previous centuries to determine the course of English economic history. This was the fourth war of a type which began with that which filled most of the reign of William III, the wars in which Great Britain, aided by a coalition of European allies, fought against France, not only in Europe, but all over the world. They had all helped to develop British industry. In the time of William III, for instance, mines had been opened up in Anglesey and Cardiganshire. But, all along, France was far more powerful than Great Britain in immediate resources. The coalition system enabled the smaller Power to develop great naval strength and to organize

alliances of Continental armies. Great Britain's own
economy served her well as the paymaster of Europe;
but that was not enough, and she financed her wars by
great borrowings from abroad.

The wars were connected with nearly all the changes
in the extent of the realm that had come about since
1662, and these were vast. In 1662 we were on the eve
of the second Dutch war. That war put an end to
most of our territorial disputes with the Dutch. In
America we gained New York and thus had a continu-
ous line of seaboard colonies from New England to
Virginia. In Charles II's reign we pushed on the
economic development of North America. Pennsylvania and Carolina were founded, and the process
lasted down to the establishment of the latest of our
mainland colonies, Georgia, in the seventeen-thirties.
Far to the North the Hudson Bay Company, another
foundation of Charles II's time, won a share of the
fur-trade in spite of French opposition. In Queen
Anne's time Nova Scotia became British for good, and
in 1759 Wolfe's victory at Quebec marked the end of
French power in Canada. In all these ninety-nine
years we had lost nothing in America except Surinam,
which the Dutch retained. In Asia our rivalry with
them had ended in something like a division of spheres
of economic action. We kept nothing in the Malay
Archipelago except a wretched post on the west coast
of Sumatra; but the Dutch withdrew from what we
now call 'India'. There our East India Company had
become a military power, though not yet a territorial
power. Here too the great contest with the French
had passed its crisis, and the English factories were
more secure than they had ever been before. On the
west coast of Africa we had acquired some trading

posts in the days of Anglo-Dutch rivalry. Since then there had been no great change, though in this war year the British had in their hands two recently captured French forts, Fort Louis (Senegal) and Goeree.

The greatest change in the realm was the union with Scotland, finally accomplished in 1707, and accomplished then because the War of the Spanish Succession made the old imperfect union intolerable. Scotland had a population of somewhere between one and two millions. In comparison with England, it was a poor country with low standards of production and consumption. Wide stretches of the Highlands were very thinly peopled, and even in the most fertile parts the standard of agriculture was not high. Edinburgh was the only town with more than 20,000 inhabitants, though Glasgow, the growing port, was approaching that number. The exports were mainly of primary products: coal was being shipped on an increasing scale; the chief export to England was that of cattle, which came south to be fattened in the Midlands. Some linen yarn was sent to England and some plaiding overseas, but the amounts were trifling. The efforts of Scottish parliaments and patriots to imitate the economic policy of richer States had been tragi-comic failures. The Union was costly to Scottish pride, and so Scottish writers made the most of such adverse effects as it had in economic life. The disappearance of the Customs barrier exposed a small and struggling Scottish fine-cloth industry to English competition, with fatal effects. A tax on salt perhaps pressed hard on the herring industry. But the Union opened the ports and markets of the English colonies to the Scots. Glasgow became an important port for the American trade: in 1718 ships owned there began to cross the Atlantic. In 1724 more than four million tons of tobacco were brought to the Clyde and three million re-exported. Industry was stimulated, most of all the linen manufacture, but also soap-works, sugar-refineries and some smaller miscellaneous manufactures. By 1760 the population of Glasgow was approaching 30,000; that of Edinburgh was more than 60,000. There was no great development of the country as a whole, but the narrow belt between these two places was astir. And England gained by the addition of these new economic partners even more than she would have gained by a like increase of population and resources within her own borders. The realm even before the Union was the most populous area in Europe within which trade was not obstructed by tariffs and other artificial barriers. It was now made much larger, with the probability of a quick development when the backward north could take advantage of the wealth and experience of the south.

Ireland, as usual, presented a contrast to Scotland: here there had been no great constitutional change, but economic relations with England had changed profoundly. The policy of colonization had failed and come to an end. The last trace of it was the settlement of some of the religious refugees from the German Palatinate in Queen Anne's time: but, long before that, English statesmen had abandoned the hope of filling Ireland with small freeholders carrying on mixed farming on the English pattern. As a class the small farmers had failed to maintain themselves and Ireland had become a country of great estates. The landlords did not run these estates as businesses; they let their land, often, except in Ulster, on terms which made for improvidence and inefficiency on the part of the tenants. The two types of farm which came to predominate were the extensive cattle farm and the spade farm. From the late seventeenth century the potato was the main food of the country, and very soon far-sighted men raised warnings about the danger of minutely subdivided holdings cultivated by men at a very low level of subsistence. Instead of colonization, the purpose of English policy, implied if not avowed, was now ascendancy: the mass of the rural population were allowed to retain their religion and their language, while a privileged Protestant class, including all the Irish who were willing to be assimilated, monopolized education and the higher offices and owned, after the war of William III, three-quarters of the land and nine-tenths of the property in the towns.

The interests of the ascendancy class were not identical with those of the governing class in England, but they had little power to assert these interests. Ireland was politically subordinate to England, and three-quarters of her overseas trade was with the larger island. Thus in some important respects English legislation dictated the course of Irish development. In the early years of Charles II's reign Ireland had a good trade in exporting store cattle for fattening in England; but some of the English squires were jealous of it, and it was prohibited. This, however, did Ireland good instead of harm, for it compelled the Irish to fatten and slaughter their own cattle, and Cork became the flourishing centre of a highly organized trade in exporting meat and butter and in victualling ships. The exclusion of Irish ships from the British colonial trade and the prohibition of the export of Irish wool and cloth to foreign markets were other examples of English protectionism, and they may possibly have prevented development in those fields; but England tolerated and even to some extent encouraged the Irish linen trade, which prospered over a large part of the country.

From all this there resulted an economy unlike that of either England or New England, with more resemblance to the sub-tropical American colonies or the poverty-stricken aristocratic countries of Eastern Europe. Dublin, the second city of the king's dominions, with a population of more than 100,000, was a brilliant capital. Its hospitals and other public institutions, its architecture and its intellectual life were in some ways better than those of London. But the country was poor in natural resources; it could neither amass capital for development nor attract it from abroad. The population grew, so far as we can tell, in an even greater ratio than in England; by 1760 it was probably in the region of three millions; but the conditions of its growth were utterly different. The new numbers were supported by the sub-division of farms and the depressing of the standard of living. In the first quarter of the eighteenth century a movement of emigration to America began. It started from Ulster, and it was connected with the legal disabilities of Presbyterians, but it was due mainly to overcrowding. Very soon everyone recognized that Ireland was miserably poor. Its economic laws and practices were criticized from every side, and in 1759 there was a first breach in the wall of British restrictions. In that war year the price of provisions in England was so high that there were riots; and the importation of live cattle from Ireland was permitted.

The population of England and Wales was now in all probability about six millions and two-thirds. Contemporaries thought it was decreasing; but we have good reason to think that, at any rate from about 1750, it was increasing rapidly. We know more about the reasons for this increase than for earlier periods, though we still do not know much. It appears to have been due mainly to a fall in the death-rate. In the late seventeenth and early eighteenth centuries social conditions in the towns appear to have been exceptionally bad, and as the eighteenth century went on there were some improvements, such as the reduction of gin-drinking, which was brought about by legislation. We have no reason to think there was any great improvement in urban housing or sanitation; but diet was probably becoming better. Another cause of better health was the beginning of the medical revolution. The worst visitation of bubonic plague in England, the Great Plague of 1666, was also the last; probably because the brown or 'Hanoverian' rat now began to drive out the black rat, the plague-carrier. That was mere good luck, but many lives were probably saved from other diseases, especially smallpox, by the improvements in medical services which began in the time of Charles II. Physicians and surgeons were amongst the most active workers in the scientific movement; they made important discoveries which influenced practitioners all over the country. Early in the eighteenth century the foundation of the Edinburgh medical school, partly under the influence of Leyden, began a reform of teaching. When the century began there were no hospitals of note in England except St. Bartholomew's, St. Thomas's, and Bedlam. Four more were added to these before 1760:

Guy's, the Middlesex, the Westminster, and the London.

In many parts of Europe, perhaps in most of the more industrialized parts, the changes in population resembled those in Britain. In some of the peasant countries there was also an increase of population about the same time resembling that in Ireland. Something of the same sort happened outside Europe: the increase seems to have been sharper in China than anywhere else, and there too, instead of promoting capitalism and industrialization, it retarded them and created a swarm of peasants. Neither in Great Britain nor in Ireland had the growth of population so far brought with it essential changes of economic structure.

The growth of London had gone on without a check. By 1760 the area governed in the twentieth century by the London County Council had somewhere near a million inhabitants: it had probably about doubled in the past century. The port had grown. By 1703 the East India Company had two dry docks and had recently opened its Howland Great Wet Dock, named after the director whose daughter had married the Earl of Bedford's heir. This could hold some 120 sail 'being much larger than the famous bason of Dunkirk or any pent water in the world'. Another cause of growth in East London was the settling of some thousands of Huguenot refugees, mainly silk-weavers, after the revocation of the Edict of Nantes in 1685. London spread westwards as well as eastwards. In the rest of the kingdom the growth of towns was so great that for the first time the provinces acquired a truly urban population. Like London and Glasgow, the other ports increased, especially those of the west. In 1662 Liverpool had perhaps 4,000 inhabitants; in

Charles II's reign the establishment of Customs officers there had to be increased; in Queen Anne's a wet dock was made; by 1760 there were between 30,000 and 40,000 people. Bristol, which was almost of that order of magnitude in 1662, was now unquestionably the second city of the kingdom, with 100,000. Norwich, in 1662 little below Bristol in size, was left far behind, though it had probably about doubled. Manchester had grown much as Liverpool had; Birmingham and Sheffield not very much less; Leeds and Nottingham very substantially, though they had not caught up with Hull. There was another thickly peopled area on Tyneside. Altogether there were nine or ten provincial towns with more than 20,000 inhabitants each.

In 1675 John Ogilby published his *Britannia*, the first road-book based on an actual survey. This was undertaken at the wish of King Charles II, and it was a sign of the interest of the Government in transport. By 1760 many of the roads had decidedly improved. The military roads and bridges planned by General Wade after the rebellion of '45 began the opening up of the Scottish Highlands. There was still no central department to look after them, but an effective machinery for development was now in use, the system of turnpike trusts. A Bill to authorize such a trust had been introduced in Parliament unsuccessfully as early as 1622; the first to become law was that for the road from London to York, passed in 1663. From the time of William III onwards others followed, and by 1760 there were toll-bars and turnpike gates, and occasional riots against them, over a great part of the country. Coach services began on the principal roads in the time of Charles II, and they had improved, though they did not cover more than forty or fifty miles a day. The royal mail coaches were on the whole the best. The posts had multiplied. Here again private enterprise played a notable part. In 1720 Ralph Allen of Bath, remarkable also as a philanthropist, began his service of posts on the cross-roads, the roads not leading to London. Over forty-four years his profits averaged £12,000 a year.

Land carriage of all kinds continued, however, to be dear; the organization of relays of horses to drag heavy vehicles was costly. With bulky and ponderous loads, water transport was still the only possible method for long journeys, and, as the use of coal in industry developed, the waterways were improved, primarily to carry the coal, but with the result that all kinds of heavy goods could now be had more easily and cheaply in the areas that they opened up. These works incorporated no new technical devices of any importance; their execution had to wait only for suitable economic conditions, especially available capital. The area of country within fifteen miles from navigable water was greatly increased. It now included almost all East Anglia. In the west the Tone had been made navigable to Taunton; in Wales and the Welsh border Carmarthen, Leominster, and Welshpool were now accessible to barges. The Kennet had been opened up and the Thames to Lechlade. The Trent had been cleared as far as Burton, the Derwent to Derby, the Idle to Bawtry. The Don was navigable to within three miles of Sheffield. There were many other improvements. Hundreds of thousands of pounds were spent on them, and almost always remuneratively. In 1744 the navigation of the Aire and Calder was let for

£3,200 per annum. But there was still room for improving transport by moving on from the simple matter of improving rivers to the more costly system of cutting canals. The first canal in England was the Aire and Calder Navigation, made in the interests of the West Riding woollen manufacture. In 1757 the great engineer John Smeaton, F.R.S., began his survey for the Calder and Hebble Navigation, to extend it to a point near Halifax. In 1759 the Duke of Bridgewater began his great undertaking, a network of canals from his coalfields at Worsley to industrial Manchester, six miles away.

The tonnage of the merchant fleet was now reckoned at 500,000, or about a third of that of all Europe. Its increase had not been interrupted by the wars; on the contrary, every war of the period had left the country with more ships at the end than at the beginning. The tonnage of the colliers had nearly doubled; that of coastwise traders in other goods more than trebled. The Newfoundland fisheries showed no great change, but the other fisheries had risen from very little to some 20,000 tons. Ships engaged in foreign trade had in 1760 some 300,000 tons, perhaps six times the tonnage of 1660. Perhaps the total of the merchant marine had grown fourfold, and Great Britain now had the largest merchant marine of Europe. The increase of shipping meant also an increase of shipbuilding and of the many subsidiary industries which contributed to the equipping and victualling of ships.

Commerce had grown and changed, but in the main in the same ways as before 1662. From 1697 the changes can be followed more easily, for with that year the Customs officials began to keep statistics of English commerce. They were neither so accurate nor so well-constructed as modern statistics, and the trade figures of almost all other countries before 1760 were even less satisfactory, and are therefore of little use as checks; but with every generation the picture becomes clearer. In the first year of the statistics the most important source of British imports was the American plantations, and seven-eighths of what they sent was accounted for by tobacco and sugar. Next came Holland, then Germany, then Turkey. The East India Company's imports came only in the fifth place, Ireland's in the sixth, then the only other substantial quantities were from Spain, the Canaries, and the Baltic. Italy sent less than Sweden alone. The order of importance was only slightly different if exports from England were considered. In this list Holland came first and the British plantations second; Ireland came fourth instead of sixth; 'Flanders' had the fifth place, but it was a war year, and we had an army in Flanders; Portugal was eighth, and after the first eight buying countries there was no single market of much importance.

In the last year of peace before the Seven Years War the total volume of trade had grown enormously, perhaps it had more than doubled. So had the trade of Europe in general, and for Britain as for Europe generally the main growth had been in trade with Asia and America. The three greatest sources of British imports were now the West Indian Islands, the East Indies, the mainland colonies in America, in that order, followed by Germany, Italy and Russia, for the Russian trade was also being opened up. Then came the Baltic, with Ireland eighth, followed by Spain, Holland and Portugal, all three of which passed on colonial goods of one sort or another to us. The list of countries to which we sent our exports was now headed by the plantations. Portugal was fourth, Ireland fifth, Spain sixth. The officials probably inflated the figures of the plantation trade, but the general result is probably correct: if imports and exports were added together, the colonies together had far the largest share. Holland's purchases of British goods had grown by something like a quarter, but her proportion of the total British exports had fallen perhaps to half what it had been. British trade had grown more rapidly than Dutch trade. The British ports were now able to short-circuit the old course of trade for East India goods, timber and grain through Dutch staples, and Britain was far stronger in manufactures than Holland. France and Hamburg were also gaining at the expense of the Dutch; but they were still rich and efficient, and still virtually monopolists in the trade of the Malay Archipelago.

The conformation of British trade had been moulded in several very important respects by protectionist policy. The constitutional arrangements for arriving at this policy were far from simple. The Ministers had under them good officials and an advisory body which took its definite shape in 1696 as the Board of Trade. Some of its members were political noblemen, but others were economic experts, and it had an efficient staff. It collected commercial information, and in its earlier years it made many important suggestions both about foreign commerce and about conditions at home. By 1760 it had settled down to a routine in which nothing of importance was transacted except in relation to the colonies, partly because the other organs of government were better able to get on without it. In trade the ultimate control was with the House of Commons, which asserted its will decisively more than once. A substantial number of the Members were leaders in the world of business, directors of the Bank of England or the East India Company, merchants and aldermen of the City of London, and there were others who could speak for particular industries, clothing, sugar-refining, or mining. Before a commercial measure became law, most of the interests concerned usually had their say in Parliament, and commercial policy therefore often included compromises between conflicting interests. That was one reason among others why it produced a very complicated, and often inconsistent, network of regulations. An eminent merchant in the late seventeenth century said that the English Customs system was 'so vast, multitudinous and by various laws perplexed that, as of a profession, it required the life of a man to be master of it'. A Customs official who wrote a guide to the subject in 1757 looked back on the intervening period as one in which 'as the laws increased, so also increased the difficulty of executing the business arising on them'.

Among the principles which these laws were meant to apply the most general and the most venerated was that of balancing the nation's annual trading account 'we must ever observe this rule, to sell more to strangers yearly than we consume of theirs in value'. It was pretty widely understood in the time of Charles II that the particular balance with one country might be unfavourable, and yet the trade with that country might contribute to a favourable general balance but in matters of policy in 1760 almost everyone still thought in terms of countries, and many regulations were meant to encourage trade with one country and discourage that with another. Of all regions the most favoured was the West Indies. They offered a large market for home manufactures, and for the slaves who were paid for by yet more home manufactures; they employed none but British shipping, their produce did not compete with our own; it was needed not only here, but also in other European countries to which we could export it, and we could buy it cheaper from them than elsewhere; for the financing of this trade, no money was sent out of the country.

The principal instrument for maintaining this relation between the old country and the new was the system of navigation laws. These were also intended—probably mainly intended—to keep up the nation's naval strength by encouraging the merchant marine, and so they not only kept foreigners out of certain branches of shipping, but they also made these branches, especially the 'far trades' to Asia, Africa, and America, artificially advantageous to the king's subjects, and they stimulated British trade with the timber-growing countries of the Baltic, the greatest source of naval stores of many kinds. The administration of the Acts did not altogether fulfil the legislators' programme even at the best of times, and there were emergencies in which they had to be suspended. So long as they kept back Run[1] the Dutch had to be allowed to bring in East Indian spices. In times of war the need for naval stores was so great that foreign crews and foreign-built ships were allowed to import them; even the rebuilding of London after the Great Fire of 1666 made such an urgent demand for timber, deal, bricks, and tiles that all these commodities had

[1] See p. 105, above.

to be freed from the restrictions. The laws did, however, succeed in guiding great masses of colonial goods into the prescribed channels. The list of 'enumerated commodities' was varied from time to time: in Queen Anne's reign molasses, rice, and naval stores were added to it; in 1722 copper and furs. It was not long before rice and sugar were virtually removed from the list by an Act which permitted them to be exported to any place south of Cape Finisterre in Brittany. The chief market for our West Indian rice was in Spain and Portugal.

From the point of view of the inhabitants of the mainland colonies, now well over two millions in number, including 500,000 slaves, the navigation laws were not very restrictive. As subjects of the king, they were entitled to many privileges under the laws, so that both inter-colonial commerce and shipbuilding flourished in Pennsylvania, New York, and New England. As early as 1726 Thames shipwrights were complaining of the competition of the colonial shipyards, and fifty years later more than a third of the British tonnage was supposed to be colonial-built. Tobacco and naval stores were the only important mainland products among the enumerated commodities: the colonists could take the rest of their products where they liked. They were not injured by the laws which directed them to fetch their European goods only from England, for the colonial trade was so much in English hands that they would probably have done so in any case, and there were exceptions to this prohibition: it did not cover salt, Portuguese wines, provisions and horses and linen from Ireland. The drawbacks on re-exports from Britain gave them some foreign goods at lower prices than the English

paid. Nevertheless, there was friction in the economic
relations of Great Britain and the mainland colonies of
the temperate zone. They were vigorous and growing
communities, with no inhibitions about evading the
laws. In 1733 a prohibitive duty was imposed to
prevent them from buying molasses in the West
Indian colonies of other European nations, but it could
not be enforced. British jealousy of their infant
manufactures led to a series of restrictive laws. In
1699 they were forbidden to carry on any woollen
manufacture, and in 1732 to export ready-made
beaver hats. At that time English business men,
especially in Bristol, were actively promoting the
manufacture of pig-iron in Virginia, Maryland, and
New England, with the hope that it might prove
cheaper than Swedish or even English pig-iron; but
they were already apprehensive of the possibility that
the colonists might go on to the further stages and
make their own bar-iron, nails, and steel. In 1750
Parliament passed an Act freeing colonial pig- and
bar-iron from all duties in Great Britain, but prohibiting all 'mills or engines for rolling or slitting iron
plating forges for working the tilt-hammer and furnaces
for making steel'.

Such efforts to keep the colonies in the position of a
'new' country were the more galling because their
standing difficulty in commerce was to find sufficient
return cargoes to pay for their European imports.
They always had to contend with adverse exchanges,
and the British Government always refused to give
them control over their own currencies, which often
suffered from many disorders. Few, if any, Englishmen in or before 1760 took a liberal view of colonial
development. The colonies were valued as markets

and sources of supply, as giving employment to shipping, as contributing to a favourable balance of trade. There was no notion of building them up as equal nations. Opinion frowned upon the emigration of Englishmen of good stock. Crimping, the forcible abduction of unwilling emigrants, was put down in the time of Charles II, and neither the export of criminals nor the fraudulent enticing of indentured labourers supplied many hands. Some of the Palatines started the excellent stock of the Pennsylvania Germans. In the main the white population of North America grew by its own natural increase.

A trade which had many attractions was that with Portugal. The Portuguese had gold to send from their mines in Africa and Brazil; their colonies were a market for our manufactures, and by the Methuen Treaty of 1703, Portugal virtually renounced the right to compete with them there or at home. It was perhaps not a valuable right, but Portugal had at that time something of a nascent textile industry. In exchange we agreed to admit Portuguese wines at one-third less duty than French wines. We saw a moment ago that Portuguese wines had also an advantage in our American market. Thus arose the classical trade of the Whig eighteenth century and its habit of drinking port wine. In 1760, however, the Portuguese trade was no longer what it had been. The minister Pombal had been for ten years experimenting in economic measures less satisfactory to England. From one-seventh of our total exports, Portugal's share had fallen to a twelfth. The flow of gold was slackening.

The Portuguese trade still kept its greatest attraction, that of being a partial alternative to trade with France. France was our nearest neighbour, the most populous

State of the Continent and the most highly civilized; but Britain traded with her as little as possible. She was the great political and colonial rival; her trade gave her the sinews of war. Apart from that she was the great manufacturing rival: she wanted to sell us either goods we could make for ourselves, especially textiles, or luxuries we could do without, such as wines and brandies. As early as 1678, at a time of political tension, the English Parliament prohibited all French imports. There was indeed a growing body of free trade opinion, associated in particular with the Tories, some of whom were friendly to France in political matters, and with the East India Company, which needed to buy its imports with bullion. The free-traders had an innings under James II; but when war with France came on under William III everything was against them and trading with the enemy was shut off more strictly than ever before. A prohibitive tariff was built up against the French. The early statisticians wrangled about the figures, but there was no denying that the French never bought from us as much as we bought from them. When the Peace of Ryswick came the Dutch made a tariff treaty with France, but we would not. At the end of the War of the Spanish Succession Queen Anne's Tory Government proposed to end the tariff war as well; but the clothiers, the Portuguese traders, the Spitalfields silk-weavers and a crowd of economic journalists carried the day against them. In 1760 the two nations were still contributing nothing to one another's prosperity. They were competing in every open market and closing every market they could control. In each there were vested interests which gained from this exclusiveness, but the nations paid dearly for them.

CHAPTER VII

LANDED WEALTH AND THE DIFFERENTIATION OF CLASSES, TO 1760

THE legislature was dominated by landlords, and it was generally believed that high rents were the best index of national prosperity. Agriculture therefore got its share of protection, and in this the corn laws were the chief instrument. About 1660 London ceased to import corn from abroad; the corn brought to market there was so abundant that it was now left to private enterprise to replenish the granaries of London, and there was soon a surplus for export. By 1689 the Dutch and other foreign merchants were ousted from the trade by Englishmen. The corn laws were altered step by step so as to leave the supplying of the consumer to look after itself and to protect the producer and the trader. First, they were allowed to export corn, however high the price might be, unless, as happened in times of scarcity, the Government put on a temporary export prohibition. Then imports were prohibited in times of plenty. In 1678 the experiment of a bounty to exporters was tried. In 1689 a celebrated Act, which had scarcely any foreign parallels or none at all, made this system permanent. It was expensive to the State. Not until 1750 was there a sound system for ascertaining the market prices on which the scale of the bounties depended. Altogether £6,000,000 were paid in bounty on corn for England and Scotland from 1697 to 1765. The net export in these seventy years was about thirty-three million quarters, which was considerably less than half of one year's production at the beginning of the period. A large proportion of this was accounted for by the ten good years from 1741 to 1750 and the five, almost equally good, from 1751 to 1755. A quarter of wheat—that is, two sacks—was supposed to be one man's food for a year, so on the average the export surplus represented less than the subsistence of 50,000 men. Even so it is uncertain whether the bounties actually caused an increase in exports in the abundant years when they were paid. On the whole, then, the corn laws had no great social effect in this period, unless it was to give some stimulus to tillage.

There were still occasional years of famine, such as 1693–9, 1708–9, 1741, 1757–9, and there was the sheep-rot in 1735 and three outbreaks of cattle plague, of which the worst was in 1758–9; but except for times like these the farms still fed the nation, even with its greatly increased population, and there was even at times a considerable export of corn and dairy produce, especially from East Anglia. It was a period of agricultural progress. The advance of improved methods from one part of the country to another cannot be traced exactly, and no doubt many farmers lagged far behind the few prominent experimentalists, the compilers of handbooks, and the advocates of foreign methods, but, so far as we can tell, diffusion of new methods went on continuously from about the middle of the seventeenth century. The Royal Society in its early days paid much attention to the matter. Better transport not only gave farmers better access to their markets, and so enabled them to grow the most suitable crops; it also brought fertilizers which overcame the deficiencies of the poorer soils.

There were many new methods in agricultural technique. The most important were those which increased the productive capacity of mixed farming by improving the rotation of crops and by making it possible to feed cattle through the winter. The growing of sainfoin and clover spread quickly in the midland and home counties. Turnips were cultivated in fields in a good many counties before the end of the seventeenth century, and this meant that the land was fertilized by sheep folded and fed in the winter on the turnips. By 1760 this had brought about a revolution in the farming of perhaps the greater part of the low land country. Along with this great change came dozens of smaller ones. Potatoes, like turnips, entered on the stage of field cultivation. Cauliflowers came in and other new vegetables. Fruit-growing was further improved. So were implements. In animal husbandry it was the same. The breeding of sheep improved as well as their feeding: in 1728 it was said that two sheep produced more wool than three or in some places four did before. The new Leicesters spread over the Midlands and the new Lincolnshire sheep over East Anglia; there were large sheep in the north-east, and the next generation saw even greater progress. Horses for various purposes were much improved in the late seventeenth century. Oxen were bred to give a greater weight of beef. Robert Bakewell, the great all-round expert on cattle, took over his father's farm at Dishley in Leicestershire about 1755.

All this did not come about without great changes in the organization of the industry—for instance, in the sizes of estates, and in the legal position of owners and tenants. We do not yet know in any detail how these changes were connected or how they varied from

one part of the country to another; but some general-
izations are possible. First, although the growth of
population was largely or mainly a growth of people
engaged in industry, both the intensification of agriculture and the extension of the cultivated area increased
employment on the land. Lands hitherto barren could
be brought into profitable cultivation by the new
methods. In 1666 a Nonconformist minister travelling
to the Spa at Scarborough saw corn growing on the
slopes of the Yorkshire wolds and exclaimed: 'Doth a
man plough upon the rocks?' Much headway was made
in the fens, marshes, moors, and forests. Thomas
Fleetwood drained Marton Mere in Lancashire in the
sixteen-nineties; John Perry stopped the Dagenham
breach and reclaimed about 5,000 acres twenty years
later; Lindsey Level in Lincolnshire was taken in hand.
The draining of the Bedford Level in the Fens entered
on a new stage of activity in 1685. The new and improved lands were, so far as we know, made available
because moneyed men, some of them engaged in
industry, rightly or wrongly expected that these lands
would be profitable if they were farmed for the
market. The increase of production was thus largely
an increase of production for marketing and not for
the subsistence of the farmers and labourers. Money
economy was not universal in rural England by 1760:
there were exceptions like gleaning in the fields
and the unpaid labour of sons on family farms;
to say nothing of the unpaid labour of wives and
daughters. But, broadly speaking, the economic life
of the country-dweller, as of the town-dweller, now
revolved round acquiring and spending a money
income.

Every kind of produce went to market, and the

F

London market drew goods from considerable distances; but the corn markets promoted agricultural change more than the others, because bread was the main article of diet. Thus although there were some instances of enclosure for pasture, they were far fewer than the enclosures of common fields for arable or mixed farming. We do not know how the enclosures of 1662–1760 compare in area with those of the previous period, but we have no reason to think they were on a much smaller scale. The years after the Restoration seem to have seen the enclosure of most of the common fields in the county of Durham, of some in Nottinghamshire, Wiltshire, and elsewhere. It was generally agreed that 'several' fields made it possible to farm better than in champion fields, and, though there are many instances of enterprise and variety among farmers in open fields, this general impression seems to have been correct. But the word 'enclosure' was 'odious to the world': it was associated with injustice to the poor, and even from the point of view of the landlord it had many inconveniences. For the first few years after the Restoration, Parliaments groped for a new policy. A number of Bills with the purpose of making enclosure easier and more certain in its effects failed to pass. Even a Bill for making more effective the statutory penalties against rick-burning or destroying enclosures was dropped because it was alleged to have been promoted in the interests of a party to a particular lawsuit.

Meanwhile, Parliament was forming the habit of dealing with enclosures by private Acts—that is by Acts not extending beyond the particular cases and dealt with a quasi-judicial procedure in which the interested parties, both for and against, had a right to be heard by committees of the Houses. There were some in Charles II's reign, a few more in Stuart times, and sixteen under George I. Then a brisk activity about the middle of the century brought the number for George II up to 226. They were equally useful to the enclosers, whether they had to do with marshes and moors or with the common arable and pasture and meadows of open-field parishes, and so it is a work of research to discover how many of the acres affected by these Acts had been seriously farmed before. The total of such lands enclosed by Act before 1760 is less than 300,000 acres out of an area of farm-lands which was probably not less than twenty million acres in England and Wales. We do not know what proportion of the open fields made way for several cultivation in this period.

Still less do we know what were the social effects of enclosures. It seems very improbable that there was any widespread depopulation. The deserted villages of poetical tradition existed, but they were not typical. It does seem, however, that the late seventeenth and the early eighteenth century constituted the critical period in the great change by which England ceased to be a peasant country and became a country with a high proportion of tenant farmers and wage-earning labourers. The enclosures seem to have helped this transition. By the late eighteenth century even in unenclosed parishes the independent peasantry of midland and south-eastern England had ceased to exist and the day-to-day direction of agriculture was in the hands of farmers, the rural middle class. The medium-sized peasant proprietors had gone and the small peasantry had been converted into wage-earners. In the great majority of open-field parishes in this part of the country the occupying owners were comparatively numerous until 1750, but they were few and diminishing in number in the parishes which had been enclosed long before. Enclosure by Act safeguarded their interests; the smallest proprietor got as good a Parliamentary title as the largest. Many writers have described the enclosure Acts as measures of expropriation carried out by a Parliament of landlords without regard for the interests of the small proprietors. In form they expropriated no one, but merely exchanged land and common-rights for new holdings of land. We know that in some instances the exchange was unfair. Many writers have assumed that it was so everywhere; but they have not advanced sufficient proofs. Detailed research on separate parishes and regions is clearing away misconceptions, and showing that sometimes no serious injustice was done; but too often this question is still discussed without any clear standard of what justice implied in terms of money and acreages. We must keep an open mind on the question whether injustice was usual or exceptional, whether the small landowners were driven out or went 'because they chose to go'.

The disappearance of the small landowner was neither complete nor equally widespread in all parts of the country. In some parts enclosure from the waste actually increased the number of small proprietors, and in others—for instance, in Lancashire and parts of the West Riding of Yorkshire—the number was probably increased by the sale and division of large estates. It is worth noting that Gregory King, though he gave the same number of freeholders of the better sort (288,000) in 1696 as in 1688, increased his estimate of the freeholders of the lesser from 120,000

to 140,000.[1] There was, however, a general tendency
for large estates to increase in size, and not only at the
expense of the peasantry. A great many of the small
gentry vanished at about the same time as the small
cultivating owners. For this there seem to have been
various reasons. After Charles II no more Crown
lands or confiscated estates worth mentioning were
thrown into the market, and the colonization of Ireland
ceased. But the same sorts of wealth which in the past
had been invested in those directions still accumulated,
and in even greater quantities: industrialization and
the commercialization of agriculture both increased the
funds seeking investment. The attractions of investing
in land were perhaps even greater than before. In
1711 an Act was passed which made the ownership of
an estate of not less than £300 a year in land a condition of sitting in the House of Commons, and,
though it was easily evaded, there are known instances
in which estates were bought for a 'qualification'. Not
only had the landed gentry the same high social status
as of old; land was still the safest of all investments and
it was of great use to the business man as security for
raising capital. In 1675 the Rev. John Dunton wrote
as follows in his 'dying' advice to his son, then a book-
seller's (or publisher's) apprentice: 'I do likewise coun-
sel you not to *sell any Part* of your Estate in Land, if
either your Wife's Portion, or your borrowing of
Money upon Interest, may conveniently serve to set
you up in your Trade.' The demand for estates was
thus at least as great as before, and now it had to satisfy
itself by buying up land which came into the market
for economic reasons. In the period of the Restoration many landowners were in difficulties, some in

[1] See the Appendix, p. 192, below.

consequence of the Civil War, others for less romantic reasons. New methods of taxation pressed hard on the landlord. When Richard Baxter in 1691 wrote his *Last Treatise*, a plea that landlords should not rack-rent their impoverished tenants, who, he said, had a worse life than unmarried labourers, he made an imaginary landlord object: 'We are kept under by taxes. . . . The maine weight lyeth on the Landlords. We have voluntarily in Parliament taken it on ourselves.' The rates of taxation may have been reasonable, but they meant that a landlord must have cash to pay with. The bad harvests in the war years of the sixteen-nineties were the worst times for farming that anyone remembered, and we know that a number of the smaller country gentry, from Northumberland to Dorset, had to sell the whole or parts of their estates at that time.

The smaller squires were probably more vulnerable than the great landowners. In several ways the law was altered after the Restoration so as to favour the great landowers. The freeing of feudal tenures in chief was an advantage to some of them. The land law was developed in such a way as to facilitate the kinds of action they wanted to take, especially 'strict settlement', which kept an estate together as a unit and enabled its holders to survive financial stresses which otherwise might have compelled them to part with their lands. The landowners, especially great landowners, 'financed the research' by which lawyers found ways round the Tudor statutory obstacles to this. In the main, however, the changes in the law, such as that which converted various tenures into ordinary tenancies 'at will', were as favourable to the small landowner as to the great, and the reasons why the great landowners relatively and literally gained ground were economic. Large funds were available for investment by creating or enlarging great estates. It was seldom that a great estate came into the market, and so whenever a small squire wanted to sell there was probably a magnate anxious to buy.

Much of the wealth by which the great estates were built up came from the ample rewards of service in Church and State, but much more came from industry and commerce. Examples may be found all over the country, though naturally in the coaching days they were commoner near the business districts. Thomas Fuller thought its proximity to London was the reason why the lands in Berkshire were skittish and often cast their owners. Some of the great landowners of the eighteenth century perhaps kept up their establishments simply from their rents; but many of them had City money to fall back on in bad times or to finance the improvements which swelled their rent-rolls. Successful business men may sometimes have put all they had into a property and then lived on it; but hundreds of them also kept an interest in business. Others transferred an interest in business to some landowner as a marriage portion for a daughter. As investment in stocks and shares became normal among the well-to-do in the course of this period, there came to be many ways in which the landowner might also be a moneyed man, and by 1760 rural and urban wealth were intermingled all over the country. Pamphleteers and politicians wrote much about the conflict between the landed interest and the moneyed interest; but it is hard to find a class of mere landlords. Defoe wrote in 1728: 'An Estate is but a Pond, but Trade is a Spring.'

The divisions of rank were still frankly related to wealth. Heralds still distinguished between 'foreign merchants' and retail shopkeepers, but they declared in the time of Charles II that 'if a Gentleman be bound an Apprentice to a Merchant or other Trade, he hath not thereby lost his Degree of Gentility'. The status of heraldry and all it stood for had sunk a little. In consequence of changes in constitutional law, the Heralds' College was no longer able to exercise a coercive jurisdiction in matters of coats of arms, and the Cavalier Parliament refused to pass a Bill for restoring this jurisdiction. The right to bear arms thus depended only on social convention, not on law. It was impossible to draw a clear line between the gentry and those below them. The upward tracks to gentility through the Church, the law, and the counting-house were more frequented than ever, and they grew broader as the nation's business grew more complicated. From the shopkeeper-craftsman through the semi-professional callings of the apothecary or the solicitor to the liberal professions and the higher commerce there were only insensible steps. Long before this time, it has been said, the English aristocracy was lateral in its emphasis—that is to say, high connexions were valued rather than ancestry. This was natural when it was easy to rise; but a strong lateral emphasis was compatible with rigid stratification, and at this time the spirit of exclusiveness seems to have been growing stronger. Gentlemen's sons were less commonly apprenticed in towns. In 1760 the stratification was not like a system of caste, but it roughly blocked out the division of functions between different groups of the community, and it did so by a division of opportunities. Inheritance was the foundation of the higher ranks and of the whole system of ownership in land and business, so that, once risen, a man had a lasting advantage, and his family with him.

But this was not the system of class divisions as it emerged later. The only class which was a class in the full sense was the governing class, with its monopoly of high public offices and its feeling of community of interest. It was graded from the great noblemen and bankers to the small squires and professional men. It was contrasted in the language of the time with the lower orders or even the lower order; but no one thought of society as consisting of three classes, upper, middle and lower. 'The middling people' were, indeed, building up institutions of their own. The important minority who were Dissenters had their chapels and academies. The rise of commerce and industry created new kinds of professional work independent of the influence of the gentry. As the numbers of wage-earners grew, employers of all kinds approached the condition of a class. The lower frontier of this stratum was, however, no more clearly defined than the upper, and the wage-earners were no proletariat. Perhaps the feature which distinguished this country most sharply from others was the strength of the working-class organizations, especially the friendly societies, which grew up over a large part of the country from about 1700 to this time and later. They had no programme of social changes. They provided sick and funeral benefits and the members managed their own affairs over a social and sometimes ceremonious pot of beer. Even the farm-labourers of many small villages had such societies, with well-constructed rules. No doubt their financial basis was often unsound and some of them were badly or fraudulently managed; but the whole movement is an amazing proof of spontaneous organization, business capacity, and mutual confidence.

CHAPTER VIII

INDUSTRY AND THE PROBLEMS OF POLICY
AND FINANCE, TO 1760

AFTER the controversy over the abortive commercial settlement with France, discussions about the monetary balance of trade played a much smaller part in the formation of commercial policy. With the growth of agriculture and manufactures, protectionism, especially in the tariff, gradually aimed more at encouraging specific industries. Even in the reign of William III there were clear signs of this. The promotion of corn exports by bounties was one. Another was the removal, a few years later, of all export duties on woollen manufactures, corn, grain, biscuit and meal, extended in 1721 to all British manufactures. This was part of a great reform of the tariff by Sir Robert Walpole which inaugurated the industrial stage of protectionism. Raw materials still had to pay export duties, or at least the important materials like alum, lead, tin, calamine, coal, leather, skins, wool-cards, and unfinished woollen cloths. The export of raw wool was still prohibited. For common-sense reasons, various import duties were reduced. Those on whale-fins, increased under Queen Anne, had ruined the 'Greenland Fishery'; those on drugs had led to an increase of smuggling; those on spices were too complicated and too high. The duties on American wood, timber, and hemp, all needed for the Navy, were abolished altogether. A drawback was allowed on many classes of silk goods exported. Walpole was not indeed able to carry out all his plans. In 1753 he proposed his 'excise' scheme, to extend to wine and tobacco the system, already successfully in operation for East Indian wrought silks, for pepper, for tea, and for coffee, of warehousing under control of the Customs so that no duty was paid if the goods were re-exported. It would have helped the growing re-export trade which was making London a great staple port; but it was violently opposed on grounds which had nothing to do with its economic merits, and Walpole had to drop it.

The re-export trade had grown out of importing from America and the East: its foundations were sugar, tobacco, Indian textiles, and China tea. Walpole and his successors had to balance the interests of traders in these goods against those of home manufacturers, and the interests of one class of home manufacturers against another. Already it was not merely a question of defending the English textile manufacturers against foreign importers, who still sent much linen cloth and yarn; there was a new problem of rivalry between wool and cotton manufactures at home. In 1760 the country was much more industrialized than it had been in 1662. Most of the important old industries were producing more and employing more hands; several of the industrial districts were more populous; there were important new industries.

The great woollen industry had indeed gone through some bad times. From 1660 for about sixty years it was chronically depressed. Its European markets were blocked by wars, by French and other competition and, from time to time, by attempts of the Spaniards, Portuguese, Austrians, and others to set up manufactures to supply their own populations. British governments brought in one protectionist measure after another; but, whenever the industry began to recover, some fresh turn in the international economic rivalry knocked it down again. From about 1720 exports began to grow once more, and by 1760 they had increased by about a third of their former amount, chiefly because the markets outside Europe were taking off great quantities. But the exports had not grown as rapidly as British exports in general; wool no longer accounted for as much as two-thirds of the total value. Internally a great change in the location of the industry had come about. Both the low prices of the bad times and the greater demand of the good times, coming as they did when inland transport was improving, accentuated the competitive advantages of the districts where efficient production was easiest. In this industry much water had always been necessary for fulling, dyeing, and other processes, and now a supply of running water with a good fall was coming to be used to drive machines for grinding logwood and for other purposes. The tough and enterprising men of the West Riding, living by their moorland becks, took advantage of this and won much of the trade of Lancashire, the Midlands, East Anglia, and the West of England. They added a larger worsted manufacture to their former range, and by 1760 they were producing or soon about to produce somewhere near half the national exports of woollen cloth of all kinds.

In Lancashire a new textile industry, entirely different in some of its chief economic characteristics, had come to the rescue. We saw that in 1662 there was already a cotton-manufacturing district. Its raw material was imported, first from the Levant and then from the West Indies. The chief centres of cotton manufacture were not in Europe, but in Asia. In that protectionist age it was therefore very difficult for

English cotton-spinners, weavers, and calico-printers to get their chance. From about 1700, however, there came a great opportunity in the growing American markets, and the African slaves were paid for partly with cotton exports. Indian cottons and muslins were imitated in England, and the calico-printing industry was firmly established before it got an unintended legislative protection from an Act passed in 1701 in the interests of wool. This Act prohibited imports of Indian printed cotton. Another Act in 1721 made it illegal to buy, sell, wear, or possess such materials, wherever made. The Lancashire manufacture, however, struggled on and in 1735 a new Act opened an easily widened gap by permitting materials of mixed cotton and linen. The slave-traders were freed from their dependence on the East India Company for cargoes, and from 1749 to 1763 India was in such confusion that there was no Indian competition in Africa. Nor was cotton the only rising industry in industrial Lancashire. The small-ware industry, making ribbons and the like, had also risen rapidly during this period, and, unlike both cotton and wool in the days of the putting-out system, it was wholly urban.

There were two industries which a long succession of projectors and politicians tried to promote in England with little success, silk and linen. The silk industry made articles of luxury which promised large profits. Silk, like cotton, had to be imported, and there were European countries with climates suitable for the cultivation of silk-worms which had developed the manufacture on a great scale and with better technical methods than those of Asia. Silk-throwing, the process corresponding to the spinning of wool and cotton, was highly mechanized in Italy early in the seventeenth century. The influx of refugees, high protection, and the grant of a monopoly to the Lute-string Company in the time of William III did something to foster the industry. It was scattered through various centres: Spitalfields for the more expensive fabrics, Coventry for ribbons, Macclesfield, Essex, Norwich. There were large employers and large work-shops even in minor centres like Canterbury. In the time of George I the Italian silk-throwing machinery was introduced and genuine factories were set up; by 1765 there were more than seven of them in different parts of the country, each employing from 200 to 800 hands. Nevertheless, silk had not risen so high as to become an export industry.

Linen was a necessity; before the rise of cotton, it was used proportionately more widely than now. There had always been a linen industry in England; and the Tudors had tried to increase and cheapen its supply of raw materials by compelling landowners to grow flax. For some reason, the Continental flax-growers and manufacturers could undersell the English, and they produced on a far larger scale. In 1663 an Act of Parliament threw open to all comers the right to make linen; here again French refugees helped, and in 1690 a privileged company was set up for making and bleach-ing linen by the French method. Women and children were set to prepare and spin flax in the workhouses. In Ireland and Scotland the industry rose in the first quarter of the eighteenth century; but in spite of every kind of protection the results were limited. In 1738 most of the counties north of the Trent still made coarse linen; but Great Britain and Ireland did not supply more than a quarter of the home consumption.

In mining and the metal industries there had been a marked advance. Coal was in demand as an industrial fuel. It was becoming harder to get. As the shallower seams were exhausted the wet period of mining began, and with it the era of serious mining accidents. Much attention was given to pumps, especially the steam-engine. In spite of these difficulties, the national output was probably trebled between 1662 and 1760, reaching something like six million tons. One of the industries which were using it now was iron-smelting. From 1735 Abraham Darby at Coalbrookdale was using coke, and this process tended to concentrate the iron industry in the coalfields. Even before that the old Wealden industry was in decline, perhaps for lack of water-power for furnaces and bellows, perhaps because its market in London was specially exposed to Swedish competition. Foreign competitors could still beat the English ironmasters. From 1718–37 imports of bar-iron increased, while home production fell; from 1730 Russia was a new competitor. It was not until the second half of the century that there was a general rise of home production. In 1760 Benjamin Huntsman was in business at Sheffield, working his great invention of cast steel; but at first his only market was in France. On the whole, however, the state of the metal industries was full of promise. The west Midlands were steadily becoming busier throughout the period, finding new markets for their buttons and firearms and heathen idols. Processes were improved and subdivided as output increased. Employers experimented with new forms of business organization. The Mines Royal and Mineral and Battery Companies maintained themselves through some vicissitudes as a vertical combination, controlling all the processes from the mine to the finished article. Sir Ambrose Crowley, a very rich man in the days of William III, migrated from the west Midlands to become an alderman of London and to control great ironworks by the Tyne. He was the prototype of the modern benevolent employer, and his code of laws for his workpeople was still in force far into the nineteenth century.

A number of miscellaneous manufactures had grown up, and many of their products are still common in our houses and in antique-shops. Paper-making had at last taken root, and the English paper-mills were now supplying not only commoner sorts of paper, but some of the finest, such as that used for Bank of England notes, which was made from 1724 by the family of Portal. The Portals were Huguenot refugees, and the large store-shed in paper-mills is still called the 'saul', from the French *salle*. Other Huguenot manufactures which came to stay were the making of plate glass for mirrors and the windows of houses and coaches, and new kinds of cutlery. There were new kinds of pottery and earthenware. At first craftsmen like Dwight of Fulham imitated the Dutch and Rhenish products, and Nottingham stone-ware was famous in the late seventeenth and early eighteenth centuries. By the middle of the eighteenth century the chief centre for the cheaper pottery for common utility was Stafford-shire, where a young man of genius, Josiah Wedgwood, started in business on his own account in 1759.

These smaller manufactures show very clearly features which are also seen in the textile and metal industries. First, although this was a period of magnificence in the decoration and all the appoint-ments of rich men's houses, the great mass of the new activity went into providing articles of everyday use

and ordinary convenience for people of moderate or
even of small incomes. In this, British industry was
unlike French. French policy had aimed at encouraging luxury trades, which needed much labour and
were very profitable even on a small scale; in many of
these France still led the world. England had taken
the other road partly because the home market, always
growing with the growth of population, and now
vigorously developed by business men, was more
stable and less exposed to foreign competition than
the foreign markets. The improvement of internal
communications made it possible for manufacturers
to disperse their products over the whole country more
cheaply and more easily: they were no longer so
dependent on fairs, and no longer confined to the
main routes between the larger towns. New classes of
middlemen passed the manufactured articles on to
pedlars and chapmen who called at the villages and
outlying farms. Manufacturers and middlemen alike
often made the round of their customers in person,
but the bagman, afterwards known as a commercial
traveller, was becoming familiar to the innkeepers
and turnpike men.

All this specialization indicated that great quantities
of goods were disposed of, and these great quantities
were provided by mechanization. Many industries
had now reached a stage in which economic changes,
whatever their direction, often led to the substitution
of machinery for hand labour. When labour was dear,
this was an obvious remedy, and labour became dearer
in the industrial districts as they became more populous, and so more dependent on food carried from a
distance, and as one growing industry competed
against another for hands. But when a depression

threw men out of work and made them compete against one another for jobs, the employers might have a new incentive to use machines, for that might be an effective way of reducing their costs.

Many, probably most, of the machines introduced in this period were not absolutely new inventions: they were brought in from Continental countries where it had been profitable to use them before England reached this stage. The ribbon-loom or Dutch loom was a complicated machine for weaving sixteen or more ribbons side by side; it had been used abroad for generations before it established itself here in the time of Charles II. So had the even more complicated silk-throwing machinery which was set up in the first English power-driven textile factory, the water-mill started by Thomas Lombe on an island in the Soar at Derby in 1718, and still to be seen there. It would be hard to distinguish the foreign from the English elements in many of the new machines used in the export industries and the others which had to contend with foreign competition, such as sugar-refining, distilling, glass-blowing, silk, tobacco, paper-making, book-printing, and timber-sawing. Perhaps even the stamping machines used in the Birmingham button and other metal work and the bolting engines used by corn-millers came in from abroad.

British technicians had, however, made five cardinal inventions which, although they had not yet been applied on a great scale, began a new stage in the industrialization of the world. First was the steam engine. The first Newcomen engine started pumping water from a mine in Staffordshire in 1712; by 1760 there were scores of them at work, but there were not yet a hundred. The steam engine was not yet used for power, except that the ironworks at Coalbrookdale used one to make an artificial waterfall. The second was the process of smelting iron by the use of coal instead of wood for fuel. The supplies of coal were not only far greater than those, already running short, of timber; they were more readily available for this purpose than those of any other country except the principality of Liége. The third invention was Kay's flying shuttle, which enabled weavers to multiply their output and so overtake the increase of the previous period, itself the result of inventions, in the supply of yarn. Fifth among the inventions of the period was a new method of producing sulphuric acid which reduced its cost to a quarter of what it had been: the first factory for this process was set up at Birmingham in 1746.

The founder of this factory was the same John Roebuck who set up the Carron Ironworks, and he was one of the typical men of the new era. The son of a prosperous Sheffield manufacturer, he had studied medicine at Edinburgh and Leyden; but he practised it in Birmingham, where he soon changed into a consulting industrial chemist. He moved in the best intellectual circle of his time, and with him the full strength of the scientific movement was applied to industrial invention. From the earliest days of the Royal Society, the scientists both in England and on the Continent had contributed to inventions in many fields. Their influence can be traced most clearly in what was purely mechanical—for instance, in clockwork and instruments of precision—but the steam engine, though it was brought to perfection by the artificer Newcomen, was the product of a whole century of accumulated scientific investigations in which Italy, France, Germany, and Holland had their parts. The first hopes of the early Fellows of the Royal Society who worked at applied science were partly disappointed; a comparatively unfruitful period set in; but by now there was a new forward movement, and applied science was coming to have a distinct organization and consciousness of its own. Once again the same tendency was at work in France and Germany; but it was stronger here, strongest of all perhaps in Scotland. It led in 1754 to the foundation of the Society for the Encouragement of Arts, Manufactures, and Commerce. Having very soon shed one of its activities when the painters hived off in the Royal Academy, this society still survives as the Royal Society of Arts.

Some of these inventions, like the pumps in mines, cleared away hindrances to work, but others meant that the same amount of work was done by fewer hands. After an interval it often happened that more work was done altogether, but the immediate result was that some workers found their employment gone. In the seventeenth and eighteenth centuries such men usually hit back without calculating whom or what to hit. The workers' response to technological improvement was often machine-breaking. In the seventeenth century they smashed ribbon-looms and saw-mills. In 1727 it was made a capital offence to wreck stocking-frames. Kay's house at Bury was sacked in 1753. But these explosions were much less significant than the beginnings of a new kind of common action by working men which began to appear as the old guilds subsided further into decay. Some new companies of this type were founded, for tin-plate and wire-workers, for the London shipwrights and watermen, for the

Witney blanket-makers; but these were exceptional and resembled employers' associations. Some of the old guilds, like the London butchers, were almost dead by the middle of the eighteenth century. The Bristol Merchant Venturers had become a sort of chamber of commerce for the city. In general, the guilds had been losing ground throughout the century before 1760. New industries grew up without any such harness. When large adjustments in the supply of labour had to be made, Parliament set aside the old monopolies of the guilds. When London was rebuilt after the Great Fire, the building trades were thrown open to all comers. At the end of the war in William III's time, as in 1660, disbanded soldiers were allowed to follow any trade. In the textile trades employers disregarded the rules against employing 'unlawful men' or taking an excessive number of apprentices. There were so many 'demarcation disputes' that we may be sure the employers in many trades were able to override the other old rules which restricted them to one narrow operation.

Combination for protecting the standard of life was of no use to the employers of the putting-out and factory systems; but it was more valuable than ever to their workmen. As the scale of industry grew it became increasingly difficult, and in many occupations it was already as good as impossible, for the journeyman to accumulate enough capital to set up on his own. Workmen who sold not the product, but their labour, wanted not, as of old, high prices, but high wages. Thus the old harmony of the guilds, in which apprentices, journeymen, and masters had a common interest in maintaining their regulations, broke up. They gave birth to half a dozen new types of organization, and by 1760 the first of these had clearly emerged, the trade union.

Early trade unionism was not a proletarian movement. It did not arise as a protest against intolerable conditions: in the early eighteenth century food was cheap, though trade was often bad. It did not arise among the lowest classes: the farm-servants, mineworkers, and general labourers were too poor and ignorant then to combine. It began where there was apprenticeship and some remains of the old guild machinery, and at first it was still the association of petty groups of workmen in a society where occupations rather than classes quarrelled, so that they often had reason to side with their employers against interlopers or against other trades. Employers' complaints against combinations 'lately entered into' began in Parliament early in the century. They had sprung up in various ways, crystallizing out from all kinds of workmen's gatherings, spontaneously improvised strikes, sick and funeral clubs, arrangements for the support of those tramping in search of work. By the middle of the century they were spreading through most of the skilled trades. They petitioned the Crown or Parliament or quarter sessions for the continuance or revival of the regulations about apprenticeship and employment, or for the maintenance of wage-rates. In 1720 the master-tailors of London and Westminster complained of a great combination of journeymen-tailors. Parliament fixed minimum wages and forbade combinations; but the combination went on and in 1744 the Government tried in vain to enforce the Act. In Devon, Wiltshire, Somerset, and Gloucestershire there were weavers' unions in the 'teens and twenties of the century, aiming at the enforcement of Tudor legislation, and in 1744 the woolcombers in the Yorkshire worsted industry were reported to have had for a number of years a union which gave benefits and tried to keep up prices.

Until the middle of the century the governing class still acted in all these matters on the Tudor principle that the industrious mechanic had a right to the customary earnings of his trade. About that time, however, a great change began. There was a clear sign of it in 1753, when something had to be done about depression among the framework knitters. After a long struggle and an exhaustive inquiry, Parliament did away with the regulations and the authority of the London Framework Knitters' Company. Three years later came another trial of strength. An Act was passed on the old model, ordering the justices of the peace to fix piecework-rates in the woollen manufacture and at the same time prohibiting combinations of workmen. In Gloucestershire the quarter sessions duly fixed the rates; but the employers protested that in the face of Yorkshire competition these rates were more than they could pay. Parliament wavered and gave in. It accepted the employers' argument for freedom of contract, and abolished the fixing of wages by justices of the peace.

Like Walpole's reform of the tariff, this change relieved some of the operations of business from State control. It is sometimes said that from about the time of Charles II's restoration, or perhaps, rather, from that of the Revolution of 1688, the State no longer had any policy for industry except that of encouraging it by protectionist measures regarding trade, and that it sank into indifference to social conditions and allowed the whole machinery of industrial control to fall into disuse. As an account of the century before 1760, this is misleading; it reads into that period much that happened later. To begin with, Parliament still legislated in many economic and social matters. The special characteristic of the legislation of this period is the number and importance of the local and private Acts, of which the enclosure Acts are the best-known group, but there were a good many public Acts throughout the reigns of the first two Georges regulating both the quality of industrial products and the conditions of employment. In 1747 justices of the peace were given a summary jurisdiction to settle disputes of 'masters and servants' over hiring and service, which seems to imply a greater interest of the State in industrial discipline. After the relaxation of the efforts of the Board of Trade there were no official reports on industrial matters which attracted much public attention, but a number of Parliamentary committees looked into them. There was not, however, as there was in France, a great staff of officials who could collect information or devise a policy of control, and therefore much of the development of business organization did not come to the notice of any State authority.

The chief example is that of the joint-stock principle. In 1720 the South Sea Bubble, an international financial crisis of the first magnitude, drew attention to the dangers of fraudulent practice in company promoting. After clearing up the wreckage, Walpole's Government protected the investors of the future by the clumsy contrivance of the Bubble Act, which strictly confined the right of joint-stock organization to companies incorporated by authority. Business was, however, expanding so generally and so rapidly that this restrictive purpose could not be fulfilled. If the law officers of the Crown would not agree to a petition for a charter, or insisted on inserting provisions which hampered the transference of stock, the promoters of a company would go to equally able lawyers and find out from them how they might carry on business without infringing the law. Thus there grew up unincorporated companies which were nominally partnerships, but which, by the use of various devices like trusteeship, had in practice all the advantage of joint-stock companies.

The metal industries and the new and growing business of insurance were amongst those which used this form of organization, under which company law, though lawyer-made and not the product of legislation, made steady advances. The principle of limited liability, already known on the Continent, was beginning to creep in—that is, the principle that the shareholder's liability to contribute towards paying the debts of the company is not to exceed the value of his holding. This removes the risk of being ruined on account of a small investment in an unsound company, and so it widens the number of investors to whom companies can appeal, and it favours the expansion of business. On the other hand, it lessens the need for investors to watch how their money is used, and it improves the chances of swindlers or optimists who use other people's money without risking much of their own. It is a powerful and dangerous principle, but it was coming in without any supervision by Parliament or the Crown.

No department of the nation's life was more radically transformed between 1662 and 1760 than finance.

The changes in public finance are the easiest to trace, because they were made by Parliament and the Government departments; but they were bound up with the changes in banking, the money market, stock and share dealing, and all the other apparatus by which the nation used money as an economic tool. As population and wealth increased, financial business necessarily became more specialized, and for various reasons it became more centralized. One of the controlling factors was the growth of Government expenditure, especially on the wars. No new kinds of peaceful expenditure of any importance were undertaken by the State. Charles II spent about £5,000,000 on the second Dutch war and more on the third; the average expenditure in the war years of William III was more than £5,000,000. The Seven Years War, which began in 1756 by costing £13,000,000 in its first year, demanded twenty-five millions in the financial year 1760–1. The modernizing of public finance began with the appointment of Sir George Downing as Secretary of the Treasury early in the reign of Charles II. He began to acquire for the Treasury some control over the expenditure of other departments and to improve its technique; but the financial revolution hardly began until the middle of the reign of William III. Until then the Government had the utmost difficulty in raising the money it needed; from that time onwards it was able to raise its revenue smoothly.

The heart of the new system was the national debt. At the beginning each war had to be paid for partly by short-term borrowing on the security of some particular taxes, the income from which was assigned to the lenders. The Government of Charles II blundered into the foundation of a long-term debt,[1] and from the time of William III some part of the expense of each war was met by loans of which the capital never has been repaid, so that the taxes have only had to meet the interest charge. In each interval of peace some attempt has been made to reduce the charge. It was not until Walpole's time that the two principal devices for this purpose, both practised long before on the Continent, were introduced, and it was not until after his time that they were highly developed: they were the use of sinking funds for accumulating money at interest to pay off the capital of loans, and the conversion of old loans at higher rates to new ones at lower. The latter method could not succeed unless the Government could borrow at a rate of interest attractive enough to investors and yet low enough for its immediate purpose. As late as 1714 it resorted to the ancient method of fixing the maximum rate of interest at 5 per cent; but ultimately it achieved its purpose by establishing a reputation for integrity.

Under William III it failed to raise the necessary sums direct from the public, but it borrowed from the Bank of England, the East India Companies, and the South Sea Company. At the end of Queen Anne's reign nearly half the debt of 36 millions was owed to these three bodies. Walpole refused to take up a plan for reducing the interest on the debt to 3 per cent: the only occasion in English history when stockholders have defeated a conversion proposal. During the War of the Austrian Succession the public had more to lend and had learnt the habit of investing in stocks.

[1] This dates from the 'Stop of the Exchequer' in 1672, when the Government, in order to finance the third Dutch war, unexpectedly retained the principal of loans made to it, but paid adequate interest.

Much more was borrowed from it direct, and after the war the companies' share of the debt was reduced and the rate of interest on some of it brought down by conversion to 3 per cent. The total debt in 1757 was £78,000,000 and in the following war years it rose sharply; but by this time British securities had such a reputation that thousands of foreign, especially Dutch, investors had bought British Government funds and Bank, East India, and South Sea Stocks. In 1762 their holdings were calculated at a little under £15,000,000 and they may have been considerably more.

Taxation, from which both the debt-charge and a part of current expenditure had to be financed, had not been modernized to the same extent as the system of debt. In one way, indeed, it had been modernized more effectively: the Government now raised all its taxes direct from the tax-payer without depending on the services of profit-making business men as collectors. In the early years of Charles II most of the taxes were paid to tax-farmers, syndicates which offered fixed sums and then made what they could by raising the taxes at the rates prescribed by Parliament. At that time there was no country in Europe which had a civil service efficient enough and free enough from corruption to do the whole of this work; but, after many experiments and compromises, first the Customs, then the Excise, and, finally, the other miscellaneous taxes were taken into the hands of the Government. This strengthened the machinery of the State, and brought it into more intimate relations with business life. There were other administrative improvements, such as the transference to Parliament of the taxing of the clergy; but there was little improvement in the taxes themselves. The Customs, as we have seen, were reformed, especially by Walpole, but they were still complicated and burdensome. The Excise too hampered trade, and Parliament was clumsy and erratic in adjusting its incidence to social requirements. There was a solitary instance of a tax imposed with the sole object of restraining consumption, the spirit duty of 1736. Walpole repealed the salt tax in order to relieve the poorer classes; but this made it necessary to increase the land tax, and the clamour of the landlords with other considerations forced him to tax salt again. This great land tax was the most notable tax of the period, but its history shows how little could be done as yet to reform the system of taxation.

The last subsidy on the Tudor model was in 1663, and after that there were various experiments in taxing the nation according to its real capacity. At last William III settled down to the land tax, which still exists at the present day as the oldest of our taxes. To begin with, it was a tax on incomes both from landed property and from other sources, but by 1760 in effect it applied only to land. Taken in conjunction with the corn laws and the regulation of trade, it meant that the landed interest was to be encouraged to grow rich in order to pay handsomely to the State. The tax was an apportioned tax. It was not only the one direct tax; it was also the elastic element in each year's finance. It was so calculated that when it was set at 2s. in the pound, the yield was £1,000,000; and as a rule throughout this period it was kept down to 2s. in peace-time and doubled on the outbreak of war. But the apportionment between different parts of the country was unscientific from the first, and became grossly unfair as the relative opulence of the counties changed with the growth of industry; commercial and industrial wealth was not tapped like landed wealth; the total amount was not enough to do away with the unfair and irritating promiscuous taxes, expensive to collect and account for, constantly increasing in number whenever the need for revenue was urgent.

Every development of public finance was accompanied by debates and pamphleteering which clarified ideas on the incidence and the social effects of taxation and investment and on money in general. The Government was actively concerned in all these discussions. It never took the responsibility for supplying the business community with all its money of every kind; but it used its monopoly of gold and silver currency as a factor in economic policy; it also issued various 'credit instruments' and Parliament prescribed the conditions on which bankers were to supply the various kinds of paper, bills, bank-notes, and so forth, by which metallic currency was supplemented and on which credit was based in home and foreign trade. In 1663 came the recognition that money was an article of commerce like the others: the export of foreign coin and uncoined gold and silver was permitted by statute. Not long afterwards the Mint ceased to make any charge for coining, so that from the official point of view the coinage became simply a part of the stock of metals. The value of the pound sterling had always concerned the Government nearly; but in this too the reign of William III began an era. A great recoinage was carried out. From that time, partly under the influence of Locke, governments accepted the view of the City men that the value of money should not be allowed to fluctuate or be deliberately manipulated according to the varying economic needs of the community, but should be kept constant.

Their way of ensuring this was to keep the pound at a fixed value in terms of the precious metals, and by 1717 this took the form of putting it on a fixed gold standard. There is no end to the theoretical arguments for and against this system; but neither is there any doubt that it conduced to the greatness of English finance in the next two generations. The foreign investor saw a safe currency. The London money market became a rival to that of Amsterdam. In the reign of William III the Stock Exchange was incorporated. After the South Sea Bubble the law and the ethics of business men kept Stock Exchange dealings on the whole to such a level of respectability that the habit of buying and holding Government securities and those of the greater companies spread all through the upper and middle strata. All over the country business men, drapers, brewers, corn-merchants, receivers of taxes, and others began to act as bankers for their neighbours, and though there were rogues and occasionally fools among them, by 1760 they were playing such a part in the seasonal ebb and flow of money between London and the provinces that there was a rudimentary banking system. The Bank of England had started as an anomalous body, in competition with others for miscellaneous kinds of business, a State bank, as one foreign observer wrote, without being in the hands of the Government. By 1760 good luck and good management had brought it to the position of being the Government's banker, the only joint-stock, note-issuing bank in England, the only note-issuing bank and the only joint-stock bank of any kind in London.

What was the relation of these great improvements in equipment and productive energy to social welfare?

There is no doubt that the benefits were widely diffused, that, with some minor exceptions, every group in the country was materially better off at the accession of George III than at the accession of Charles II. We may take as a first test the spread of what were regarded as luxuries. In 1664 the East India Company gave King Charles as a present 2 lb. of tea. The regular importing of tea began in 1670, and the direct import from China in 1689. The amount imported was increased, and so the drink was popularized, by the rivalry between the Old and the New East India Companies in 1698–1707, and in that period 'it descended to the plebeian order amongst us'. The progress was interrupted by depressions; but it was always resumed, and by 1760 it was a bad year when less than three million pounds came in. It was not yet much used by the wage-earners; but among all others it was very common. The use of sugar had gone up in a similar way: in 1700 about 10,000 tons were imported; in 1760 about six times as much. So it was with tobacco. We cannot give figures for the consumption of wheaten bread, but it was certainly much commoner. The farmhouses, the cottages, the houses of workmen and tradesmen in the towns were larger, more solid and better furnished. There were still many one-roomed houses in the remote north and north-west, and chairs and curtains were still scarce among labourers; but, except that in London the increased population had caused an increase of slum conditions, there was a general improvement of housing. Any reasonable test that we can apply—such as a comparison of the cargoes moved along the inland waterways—shows a general rise in the standard of living. Modern studies of prices and wages lead to the same conclusion.

G

During this period the poor law continued to occupy much the same place as before. The chief novelty was that humane people were disturbed about the sufferings of poor law children who were apprenticed to cruel masters, a common experience now that industry demanded more cheap labour. There had been such cruelties long before, and they attracted little attention if the parents were to blame; but it was felt that the public were responsible for the poor law. Nobody was proud of the poor law, or even satisfied with it; innumerable pamphleteers suggested changes, and Parliament took an active part, but the results affected law and machinery rather than the economics of the system. The Board of Trade in John Locke's days collected materials for a codification of the law, but Parliament never found time for this. Public finance was difficult then, and many people thought the country was spending too much in poor relief. The Board tried to discover the amount: a very imperfect set of returns collected from the parish clergy formed the basis of their estimate of £400,000 a year. This was much less than some of the current estimates, but it was a large figure. Parliament favoured the idea, in which various economists and philanthropists agreed, that expenditure on poor relief could be made to pay. If parishes were combined in large units, they could set the poor to remunerative work. Private groups, including the Quakers of London and Bristol, carried out encouraging experiments, and the early eighteenth century saw the decline of the old parish poorhouse and the rise of the workhouse. Before that time a workhouse meant a factory; now it came to mean something intermediate between an almshouse and a prison, run with the hope, generally delusive, of profit. Willingness to be lodged in it was used by some parish authorities as a test of the right to receive relief, and an Act of 1723 authorized this 'workhouse test' as the general law of the land. This was one of the main reasons why in later years the poor law was complained of, not merely as corrupt, but as harsh and oppressive. Other changes in the law, by tightening up administration and accentuating the element of discipline, tended to the same result. Perhaps they reduced expenditure.

The discussions of the politicians and pamphleteers showed deep divisions of opinion and raised some great problems of economics. There were some who could see that there were 'many thousands whose necessities are very great, and yet they do what they can by their honest labour to maintain themselves; and many times they would do more than they do but for want of employment'. Some of the economists thought that the workhouses reduced wages and so facilitated production; others thought they increased unemployment; all agreed that the mere giving of relief outside the workhouse reduced the supply of labour. Some thought that wages depended on supply and demand, others that they varied with the cost of living; almost all agreed that low wages meant cheaper production and so favoured our competition with the foreigner in export markets. Only exceptional writers could see that the home market too was remunerative to the nation, and hardly any understood that the growth of the home market was an essential part of the rising prosperity which enabled the nation to carry its burden of poverty. The curious idea was widely accepted that a large part of the work done in the country did not contribute to the nation's wealth. The movement of ideas was by no means altogether in the direction of 'economic liberalism'. The whole poor law itself, like the workhouse, was a State institution interfering with the free supply and demand for labour; but it was thought of as operating outside the productive community. It could be truly said 'the laws render the Poor more bold, when they know the Parish Officers are bound either to provide them work or give them maintenance', and so this provision which had begun as Christian charity now caused many of the prosperous to look on its recipients with aversion.

A few years before the point we have now reached, Edmund Burke published his first book, an ironical book which still puzzles commentators who try to interpret its purpose. It has a terrible paragraph about economic misery: 'We scarce believe a thing when we are told it, which we actually see before our eyes every day without being in the least surprised. I suppose that there are in Great-Britain upwards of a hundred thousand people employed in lead, tin, iron, copper and coal mines. . . . An hundred thousand more at least are tortured without remission by the suffocating smoke, intense fires, and constant drudgery necessary in refining and managing the products of those mines. If any man informed us that two hundred thousand innocent persons were condemned to so intolerable slavery, how should we pity the unhappy sufferers and how great would be our just indignation against those who inflicted so cruel and ignominious a punishment!' No long time was to go by before pity and indignation among the fortunate, resentment and rebellion among the victims, filled the world with noise and movement; but Burke wrote these words for a governing class which enjoyed deep social peace and had no sensitive social conscience.

We have followed through nearly 300 years some of the changes by which the peasant country of Henry VII has become the England that we know. We have reached a point much nearer in time to the present day than to our starting-point, but far greater changes have come about since 1760 than those that we have reviewed. Some of them had begun already and went further: the scientific revolution, the medical revolution, the financial, agrarian, and industrial revolutions went on with gathering momentum; population grew; its distribution altered with the changes in industry and transport; trade cycle followed trade cycle; the differentiation of classes proceeded on its course. But there were also new beginnings, reversals, and full stops. The great Empire of 1760, and the economic system founded on it, were disrupted, to be followed by new empires and new systems; the increase of population has slowed down; the long advance towards free markets and 'income economy' has come to its term; the tendency towards economic liberalism seemed to become a general advance in that direction, but ended in a retreat to controlled economy. If we are seeking the genesis of the economic world of to-day, we must go on beyond 1760, and we must expect surprises.

From another point of view, we may well stop at 1760. If history has no visible beginning, neither has it any end. No historical book can ever come down to the present, for as the ink dries on the last written word, the present is past. In yet another sense history is always ending: every minute is the end of it for

someone who dies, and there were plenty of Englishmen who earned their livings and paid their bills in
1760 but never saw 1761. Halting, therefore, at this
chosen point, we may look back over the changes we
have traced. We have seen how complicated they were,
not forming a simple process, but resulting from the
interdependent conflicts of opinions and interests in
which groups, districts, trades, industries perpetually
shifted their alliances and alternated between rivalry
and co-operation. We have also seen that there is no
firm borderline marking off economic affairs from
politics, religion, science, education, and all the other
aspects of human life. All along we have had to take
into account, not only the affairs of this country, but
more and more of the outside world. But through all
this there has been a central theme.

There was a difference between the events at home
and those abroad. When Englishmen dealt with
foreigners, whether doing their private business or
negotiating for the State, they followed calculations
of advantage, restrained to some extent by their moral-
ity or their sympathies, but not as they dealt with
Englishmen. Their government owned a direct responsibility for the welfare of its own subjects, and
however selfish or partial the governing class may have
been, it could not have continued to govern if it had
not accepted this special relation to them and to them
alone. They too, when they dealt with their own
countrymen, took much for granted that they could
not assume with foreigners. When men speak the same
language, have grown up under the same institutions,
resemble one another in habits and enjoyments and
prejudices, they find it easy to judge one another's
characters and fit in with one another's intentions.

In other words they form a community, and English economic history is part of the history of a national community.

These are all differences of degree, not eternal differences of kind. The English community did not remain unaltered either in extent or character, and it was never simple or uniform. Henry VII had subjects who spoke French, Cornish, Welsh, and Erse, and there was far more diversity of economic interest among them than of language. They were bound together by customs and institutions which decided who were to have authority and on what occasions there was to be discussion before they should act on their authority. Even then there were innumerable matters which were settled by the special kind of discussion that we call 'bargaining', and we have seen how its sphere extended under the control of law. By the time of George III it had brought into being a business nation, with a network of new institutions, joint-stock companies, banks, insurance companies, trade unions, binding the community together in new ways. Their growth had not been easy or harmonious; but although the poorest were still miserably poor, comfort and well-being had spread, if unevenly, through all the land. Centuries of common experience had produced men who knew how to work together, skilled and adaptable craftsmen in town and country, city men with an instinct for the touch of the market, sea-captains disciplined and adventurous. The wealth of England was in their hands and brains.

GREGORY KING'S TABLES

[See p. 157, above]

GREGORY KING drew up a number of tables of the population and economic resources of England and Wales in the late seventeenth century. They do not all inspire confidence; his estimates of a million rabbits and 24,000 hares and leverets must be guesses; but where methodical work was possible, his method was good. He made a house-by-house survey of the parish of Harefield in Middlesex, which ought to be published. The following table exists in two versions, of which one is sometimes described as a garbled version of the other. In fact, they were made at different dates, and possibly the later differs from the earlier partly because King thought the facts had changed. The figures given below are for 1688, except those in square brackets which are for 1696. It should be noted that 'families' means households, and includes not only domestic servants but apprentices and other employees 'living in'.

Number of Families	Ranks, Degrees, Titles and Qualifications	Heads per Family	Number of Persons	Yearly Income per Family £
160	Temporal lords	40	6,400	3,200 [2,800]
26	Spiritual lords	20	520	1,300
800	Baronets	16	12,800	880
600	Knights	13	7,800	650
3,000	Esquires	10	30,000	450
12,000	Gentlemen	8	96,000	280
5,000	Persons in greater offices and places	8	40,000	240
5,000	Persons in lesser offices and places	6	30,000	120
2,000	Eminent merchants and traders by sea	8	16,000	400
8,000	Lesser merchants traders by land	6	48,000	198 [200]

Number of Families	Ranks, Degrees, Titles and Qualifications	Heads per Family	Number of Persons	Yearly Income per Family
				£
10,000	Persons in the law	7	70,000	154 [140]
2,000	Eminent clergymen	6	12,000	72 [60]
8,000	Lesser clergymen	5	40,000	50 [45]
40,000	Freeholders of the better sort	7	280,000	91 [84]
120,000 [140,000]	Freeholders of the lesser sort	5½ [5]	660,000 [700,000]	55 [50]
150,000	Farmers	5	750,000	42 10s. [44]
15,000 [16,000]	Persons in liberal arts and sciences	5	75,000 [80,000]	60
50,000 [40,000]	Shopkeepers and tradesmen	4½	225,000 [180,000]	45
60,000	Artisans and handicrafts	4	240,000	38 [40]
5,000	Naval officers	4	20,000	80
4,000	Military officers	4	16,000	60
50,000	Common seamen	3	150,000	20
364,000	Labouring people and out-servants	3½	1,275,000	15
400,000	Cottagers and paupers	3¼	1,300,000	6 10s.
35,000	Common soldiers	2	70,000	14
	Vagrants, as gipsies, thieves, beggars, &c.		30,000	
		Total	5,500,520	

BIBLIOGRAPHY

THE best modern text-book is E. Lipson, *Economic History of England*, 3 vols. (i, revised, 1937; ii and iii, 1931). W. Cunningham, *Growth of English Industry and Commerce*, 3 vols. (5th and 6th ed., 1910–19) is still useful. In 1927 Mr. Lipson founded the *Economic History Review*, which publishes valuable lists of new books and articles, and is indispensable for the study of English economic history. Research is so active that many of the accepted ideas are undergoing revision. All that can be done here is to mention a few standard books. Much of the best modern work is in monographs on particular industries or regions, and every student would do well to begin with the history of some town, village, county, trade, or profession of which he has first-hand knowledge. There are so many of these that a representative selection cannot be given here: many are named in two volumes of the *Bibliography of British History*, *Tudor Period*, by C. Read (1933) and *Stuart Period*, by G. Davies (1928) and in Judith B. Williams, *Guide to the Printed Materials for English Social and Economic History*, *1750–1850* (2 vols., 1926).

The best general approach to the period we have treated is to read Adam Smith's *Wealth of Nations*, first pubished in 1776: the edition in two volumes by Edwin Cannan (1904) is a model of what such an edition should be. It is useful to compare Smith with some such recent book as E. F. Heckscher, *Mercantilism* (2 vols., 1933). For the legal framework the best book is Sir William Holdsworth, *History of English Law* (12 vols. and Index, 1922–38). For the poor law and all questions touching local administration, the great work of Sidney and Beatrice Webb, *English Local Government* (vols. i-vii, 1906–22) should always be consulted; the same authors wrote the standard *History of Trade Unionism* (new ed., 1911). In spite of many imperfections, J. E. Thorold Rogers, *History of Agriculture and Prices* (vols. iii-vii, 1882–1902), is still the chief work of reference for prices; it is to be hoped that it will be superseded by the elaborate *Prices and Wages in England*, of which the first volume, by Sir William Beveridge and others, was published in 1939. Modern methods of study in this field are exemplified by Elizabeth W. Gilboy, *Wages in Eighteenth Century England* (1934).

The best book on commercial policy under the early Tudors is G. Schanz, *Englische Handelspolitik gegen Ende des Mittelalters* (2 vols., 1881); for the period of James I there is Astrid Friis, *Alderman Cockayne's Project and the Cloth Trade* (1917). A very important book is W. R. Scott, *English, Scottish and Irish Joint-Stock Companies to 1920* (3 vols., 1911–12). It has no continuation except on the purely legal side, for which A. B. du Bois, *The English Business Company after the Bubble Act, 1720–1800* (1938), is valuable. For tables of foreign trade from 1696, which must be used with caution, Sir Charles Whitworth, *State of the Trade of Great Britain* (1776), is useful. P. Mantoux, *The Industrial Revolution in the Eighteenth Century* (1928), is very good.

The three leading English economic historians of the generation after William Cunningham have been George Unwin, Sir John Clapham, and R. H. Tawney. Among their works are Unwin's *Studies in Economic History* (1927), Clapham's *History of the Bank of*

England (2 vols., 1944), and Tawney's *Agrarian Problem in the Sixteenth Century* (1912) and *Religion and the Rise of Capitalism* (the 2nd ed., 1937, should be used). The last-named is a controversial book, and the controversy still goes on.

A sketch of the history of nutrition is given by J. C. Drummond and Anne Wilbraham, *The Englishman's Food* (1939); the most thorough study of any part of this subject is Sir William Ashley, *The Bread of our Forefathers* (1928). For public finance, A. E. Feavearyear, *The Pound Sterling* (1931), W. Kennedy, *English Taxation, 1640–1799* (1913), and E. L. Hargreaves, *The National Debt* (1930), are useful. The economic applications of science are discussed in G. N. Clark, *Science and Social Welfare in the Age of Newton* (1938). Finally, mention may be made of some among the many other books that have been drawn upon in these pages: N. S. B. Gras, *The Evolution of the English Corn Market* (1915); C. S. and Christabel S. Orwin, *The Open Fields* (1938); T. S. Willan, *River Navigation in England, 1600–1760* (1936) and *English Coasting Trade, 1600–1750* (1938); D. Knoop and G. P. Jones, *The Medieval Mason* (1933); J. U. Nef, *The Rise of the British Coal Industry* (2 vols., 1932); M. J. Bonn, *Die englische Kolonisation in Irland* (2 vols., 1906).

INDEX

Printed in Great Britain by The Camelot Press Ltd., London and Southampton

5. 46